School Development and the Management of Change Series: 5

The Management of Change in the Primary School

Implementing the National Curriculum in Science and Design Technology

Anne Pennell
David Alexander

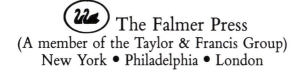

The Falmer Press
(A member of the Taylor & Francis Group)
New York • Philadelphia • London

UK The Falmer Press, Rankine Road, Basingstoke, Hampshire, RG24 0PR

USA The Falmer Press, Taylor & Francis Inc., 1900 Frost Road, Suite 101, Bristol, PA 19007

© 1990 Anne Pennell and David Alexander

First published 1990

British Library Cataloguing in Publication Data
Pennell, Anne
 The management of change in the primary school: implementing the national curriculum in science and design technology. — (School development and the management of change series; 5).
 1. England. Primary schools. Curriculum. Planning and development
 I. Title II. Alexander, David III. Series
 372.19′0942

ISBN 1-85000-540-0
ISBN 1-85000-541-9

Jacket design by Caroline Archer

Typeset in 10½/11½ Bembo by
Chapterhouse, The Cloisters, Formby L37 3PX

Printed in Great Britain by Taylor & Francis (Printers) Ltd, Basingstoke on paper which has a specified pH value on final paper manufacture of not less than 7.5 and is therefore 'acid free'.

The Management of Change
in the Primary School

School Development and the Management of Change Series

Series Editors: Peter Holly and Geoff Southworth
Cambridge Institute of Education
Cambridge, CB2 2BX, UK

Contents

To Eileen and Fred

Acknowledgments

In writing this book we acknowledge the thanks which we owe to the many headteachers and teachers in Bedfordshire and the other LEAs with whom we have worked. Without realizing it, they have acted as the source for the development of the ideas which we have outlined.

We are grateful for the support and encouragement given to us by Bedfordshire LEA and all of those colleagues who have contributed to the production of this book, without whom we would not have been able to achieve the progress made to date.

Authors' Preface

This book is about the activity which needs to take place both in schools and LEAs in order to educate young people for the future. Activity, in this sense, means physical movement and mental agility on the part of teachers who provide for the actual needs of children both in the broader sense and also at a particular point in time. The development of an understanding by the teacher of how children acquire their learning and how teachers, schools and LEAs can provide for that learning to take place along the guidelines provided by the National Curriculum is a central theme. An attempt has been made to describe possible models to help this important process work.

The book is written in two sections. Firstly, a strategy which has been used in one LEA to implement change in the primary phase. Secondly, a collection of exemplary school-based workshop material which has been tried and tested out on many in-service occasions with groups of teachers.

The book has been written with three audiences in mind, the LEA, the headteacher and the classroom practitioner. An attempt has been made to make each chapter 'free-standing' so that it can be read in isolation for a particular purpose. Alternatively, particular chapters might be selected according to the needs of the readers. Of course, it is important when using the book in this way, always to keep in mind the total model, so that the improvement process has purpose and leads in a particular direction. Chapter 1 gives an overview of the whole book.

PART 1:

The Management of Change

Chapter 1

How It All Began

It is all about a group of individuals using what they know intelligently, taking responsibility for their actions within a collective enterprise and working hard, very hard, together towards a common goal.[1]

David Hopkins, 1987

Much recent research has featured the process of curriculum development; few people, however, have attempted the less esoteric task of describing in writing the activity surrounding the implementation of a change process. The activity may be easily described but to persuade another individual or group of people to devote some time and effort to the task of change is more difficult. Yet that is the main purpose of this book; to persuade headteachers and teachers that positive development and change is within their grasp and can be very exciting.

Certainly, with the requirement for all schools to implement the National Curriculum, developmental change is a process with which all schools must come to terms. As one of the 'core subjects' of the basic curriculum, the teaching of science will need to be given priority. Much progress has been made by some schools and developments in science and design technology are underway. Much of that which has gone before can be treated as a learning process; one on which the requirements for the future can build. The experience which is now described has formed the basis for the developments in one authority.

At the outset various forms of in-service courses were established based mainly on the work of the Schools Council Project, *Science 5–13*. Resources were provided to help schools develop an investigative approach to learning but, although most teachers attempted to use them, few were able to effect, in an imaginative way, the acquisition of learning through experience by young children. Obviously the provision of courses and resources helped, but few teachers appeared to be able to develop beyond a descriptive approach to science through natural history. Very few primary teachers wanted to be involved with the physical side of science. Clearly a way of boosting the confidence of experienced primary practitioners was needed if progress was to be made. Impetus to the development was given by the first major survey of Primary Schools by HMI which was published in the autumn of 1978. The opening sentence in the science section of the survey was: 'Few primary schools visited in the course of this survey had effective programmes for the teaching of science'. This proved stimulus enough to find ways in which science could be implemented as a permanent fixture in the primary curriculum in Bedfordshire.

At first tentative discussions were set up informally between those people employed by the LEA whose work was external to schools but who visited primary schools on a regular basis. For example, advisory and college of education staff. Quickly it was found that the language being used to express ideas about science and its interpretation to younger children was not always common among members of the small group. Similarly, when colleagues representing the primary phase were invited to join the group, a second series of discussion meetings was necessary in order to refine this common vocabulary thus ensuring that, when visits were made to primary schools, everyone was giving the same message to headteachers and teachers. Although this may seem a fairly obvious process it proved to be a most important one, not only in terms of the outcomes in schools but it also provided the group with a focus for discussion and the necessary motivation and momentum to continue to develop.

At a later date this informal group became known as the Primary Science Review Group. Later still the group, consisting initially of advisory and college of education staff, was enlarged to include wardens of teachers' centres, headteachers and teachers. The review process took the form of sharing information about developments, advising on the resource needs of teachers and discussing the forms of in-service provision needed to initiate and sustain the change process. The review group continued its work until about 1985 when the Educational Support Grant (ESG) project was set up in primary science. The work of the project quickly overtook the function of the review group, though the ESG group still continues to derive its momentum from the provision for and observation of classroom activity.

Until the late 1970s a similar pattern of in-service provision to that which was being provided by all other LEAs was to be found. Through secondments and attendance at short courses, usually provided by 'experts' who talked with enthusiasm about science as a subject, it was assumed that teachers would then be capable of modifying the material to provide experiences for younger children. In practice it was only one or two teachers who were able, usually in the confines of their own classroom, to provide activities from which children learned first-hand about the interesting world around them. Some of the projects developed nationally by the Schools Council and others also helped to build up a momentum at this time. The success, measured in learning outcomes for the children, remained largely in the hands of individual teachers, only a few of whom had an effect on the development of science throughout the school. The extent of curriculum continuity in science for primary aged pupils was therefore difficult to assess.

The main driving force of the development which has taken place during the past decade or so was the improvement of the science content of the primary curriculum. It was, however, recognized at a very early stage of the development that many of the ideas being tried out had general application to most of the subjects taught in the primary school. Often it was found, during these early stages, that the need for language skills, particularly vocabulary acquisition, and the practical skills learned in mathematics, were to prove motivational to the teachers, since they could be achieved through the development of the science curriculum. From these observations the authors learned much about the change process and were encouraged by the small successes which appeared to be taking place in thinking and practice.

What then was done to build upon this experience and embark upon the change process? How was the desired change managed? In an attempt to answer these questions, each of the seven main ideas expressed below will be expanded upon in subsequent chapters. They may then be read in isolation should the reader feel that his/her particular needs can be met by so doing.

Early on the schools involved in trying out ideas generated by the Review Group were chosen on a self-selection basis. If a clear need could be identified and there was a willingness on the part of the head and staff to enter into a 'contract' for change, then time for development on a trial basis was set aside. As time passed schools were selected more systematically; groups of schools in particular areas of the county were invited to become involved with the process. Just as during the initial stages it was clear that there was a need for policy to be developed within the LEA, it became obvious that each school participating in this development needed to formulate its own policy for science education. Fortunately, at this time the Schools Council Project, *Learning Through Science*, was working on this very question. Two groups of teachers were asked to join in the discussion initiated by the project and the results, along with those of other groups working in other LEAs, were sent back to the central project team for evaluation and subsequent publication.

All of this early work with schools indicated beyond doubt that the recipe for successful change lay within the school itself. Taking the course to the school and designing the programme to meet felt needs resulted in the provision of the opportunities for some teachers, some of whom had never attended a course in their lives, to contribute positively to the development of the curriculum of their own school. All this was achieved through workshop activity relevant to the needs of the school, developing the activity from one session to the next by trying things out in the classroom, and holding discussion meetings during twilight hours in school.

The result of this way of working was that the staff involved developed a feeling of ownership of the process, but there was also a negative side which came through on certain occasions. The exposure of weakness and sometimes the inability to trust each others' judgment of situations often put a strain on relationships. These situations, when they developed, highlighted a second important factor, the value of the support of someone outside the school. An external change agent who could act immediately so that the difficulty was never left to get in the way of a major development ensured continuation. It was not uncommon for one of the team to spend many hours with a headteacher discussing in great detail the nature of the problem and how it could be put right. It was a time-consuming process but absolutely essential to the growth of change in the school and in developing ideas within the LEA.

The jargon phrase, 'external change agent' has just been mentioned. It is used as a generalization to describe all those people and institutions who can be called upon by the school to help with the change process; it could be a parent or a university professor. The essential point to make in connection with external change agents is that ideally the school should determine when they should be employed and for what reason. The importance of a strong supportive mechanism, internal and external, to school during the process of change cannot be overemphasized. In short, schools develop internally, through the commitment, leadership and enthusiasm of the staff supported by external help, as Holly and Southworth (1989) also argue.

The third element was the development of the so-called Bedfordshire Model for Change, based upon work by an American team, Lippitt *et al.*, in 1958. The original model, described in the paper by Alexander and Pennell in 1981, has been subsequently refined and simplified. The simplified version of this model is outlined in chapters 5 and 6. However, it can briefly be described as a management model for development which, when applied flexibly, acts as a mechanism for change to take place. It also recognizes that change must be introduced gradually through a number of well planned temporary stages, so that the teachers' confidence, when trying things out which are unfamiliar, is maintained. Too many good ideas have been killed in the past because teachers have felt threatened or have feared that they might lose control when trying something new.

The fourth factor, effective management of the change process in school, cannot be over-stressed. Initially this involves finding out what needs to be done. Should a school then decide to commit itself to change to develop science and technology and use the framework model, it will soon become apparent that planning is a necessary pre-requisite before action takes place. Furthermore, when the goals agreed by the group are clearly being reached, the morale of all concerned is raised. Such success is very rewarding and almost invariably leads to an increased motivation and commitment not only to the change process, but also towards the practical everyday task of teaching and learning. Another requirement which soon becomes apparent is the need for those concerned to share the tasks and responsibilities; or, put another way, the particular roles of those involved with development must be agreed.

Related directly to this, a fifth component in implementing an LEA policy for the development of primary science and design technology is the need for effective leadership within the school and this will be commented upon in more detail later.

The sixth element to support change is the provision of resources. A major problem in the development of a practical approach to learning through science and design technology is the provision of materials to aid a particular activity. It may be something as sophisticated as a thermometer or as simple as a safety pin; each item in its own way may be crucial in its contribution to the learning process at a point in time. Without any doubt whatsoever, if teachers themselves were asked for their opinion on what is needed to help them provide for change, they would all respond in the same way and ask for material support.

Crucial to the support of all that which is described briefly above is the development of appropriate programmes of In-Service Training or INSET. In recognition of this training need, the resources provided nationally through the Educational Support Grant scheme were put to good use. The ability to support centrally-based staff, to work from the Centre for Primary Science and Technology, meant that the previously modest rate of development could be accelerated. This additional resourcing came at a time when the earlier necessary groundwork had already been completed and all was ready to expand.

More recently the Consortium arrangements for school-based activities under the Grant Related In-service Training (GRIST) package have enhanced possibilities even further. Increasingly taking a county-wide perspective, schools aware of and involved in the process of change are organizing for themselves another form of support. They are joining together with other schools in localities which are engaged upon similar forms of development. When this begins to happen, it is a healthy sign that innovation is spreading from school to school, leading to permanent change. So the two government initiatives, ESG and GRIST, supported by the Local Education Authority have been timely in their arrival.

Lastly developmental initiatives need to be accompanied by inbuilt evaluative strategies. Evaluation must not become an afterthought or something which is applied to an initiative when it is considered to be completed. Rather, evaluation should be achieved through the development of critical self-awareness which is noted and discussed in an open, honest way within the group involved. It is then and only then, that the change process, accompanied by an attitudinal change on the part of those involved, begins slowly to take place. Although the subjects under discussion are science and design technology it must be apparent by now that the model for change is not subject specific; it can therefore be used as a strategic framework for any process involving change.

The seven ideas described above can exist in isolation without any connections being made. It is only when the elements are recognized clearly and a strategy for change applied, that a school begins to embark on a process of improving itself.

Finally, to round off this introduction, perhaps it is appropriate to write a few words about the current situation. Much strength, insight and inspiration has been gained from the many projects which have, over the years, researched into the development of science at the primary stage: *The Nuffield Junior Science Project*, Schools' Council's *Science 5–13, Learning Through Science, Match and Mismatch* and the APU, to name but a few. More research is needed which is classroom focused and concentrates on the way in which young children begin to acquire learning. The acquisition of knowledge and development of concepts and skills are still very important and will no doubt dominate most of the child's time through the system. Attitudes and values, which hitherto have been neglected, will assume a much more central place in the curriculum as a whole. Sex stereotyping begins at a very early age in our society, this aspect of a child's development, together with many more attitudinal changes needs to be raised to even higher levels in the consciousness of the teaching profession. In addition, the importance of the greater recognition, backed by increased resource support, of the needs of the primary phase of education needs to be established.

With the advent of the National Curriculum, all schools are being required to undergo change and development of some kind. Those schools which hitherto have not tended to become too involved with the teaching of science are having to address the issue. Change applied to a school as a whole is a difficult and delicate process, one which needs to be handled carefully. The description which follows in the rest of the book is based on real experiences over a number of years working with many schools and teachers; they are passed on to help others who need to embark on a process of curriculum change.

Note

1   Hopkins, D. (Ed.) (1987) *Improving the Quality of Schooling: Lessons from the OECD International School Improvement Project*, Lewes, Falmer Press, pp. 196–7.

Chapter 2

What Do We Mean by Primary Science and Design Technology Education?

Introduction

Gavin, who is ten years old, had difficulty in coming to terms with some aspects of the curriculum, language and number in particular, and his written work also left much to be desired. He did, however, develop a fascination for insects whilst following a class topic on 'mini-beasts' and his teacher was able to use this interest as a learning focus. One day he was busy looking after his stick insects when he paused for thought: 'You know Miss, I think we're being cruel to them — somebody said, the other day, that they liked yellow privet best and we only give them the green sort.' His teacher asked if he was sure about this, whereupon Gavin proceeded to find an answer to the problem for himself. Later, a friend of the family promised him some locusts if he could find appropriate accommodation for them and this stimulated him, with the help of his teacher, to set about designing and making a locust cage.

Above all, primary science and design technology education should involve children in first-hand investigation and practical problem solving in the natural and man-made world around them: in Gavin's case, not only in investigating the problem of food choice in the natural world but also in solving the accommodation problem in the man-made world. As well as being relevant to everyday life, the work should also be meaningful and, as far as possible, of particular interest to the individual concerned, as it was with Gavin. Children who are involved, as by-standers, in solving an orchestrated problem which the teacher engineers are being deprived of a meaningful science and design technology education just as surely as those who are given a recipe-style science work card or technology brief to follow or, at worst, set to work from books which require no practical activity whatsoever. In these circumstances, even if the work is practical in nature, it may not involve first-hand experience and, most importantly, the children are not really being given the opportunity to try out their own ideas, since they merely follow a series of closed written or oral instructions. Whereas it is recognized that, unlike Gavin, children are not always capable of formulating their own problems, it is crucial that, within the chosen topic area, the work cards or technological briefs used should be open-ended enough to allow the teacher to discuss possible lines of investigation with individuals or groups of children. Each should be given the opportunity to select aspects of the topic which motivate them and try out their ideas first-hand within the constraints of the school environment and their own abilities.

Objectives for Science and Design Technology Education

Having discussed the importance of allowing children to investigate at firsthand, towards which main objectives should teachers be working? As well as developing skills such as designing and making and problem solving, children should be encouraged to develop certain personal qualities, ideas or concepts and acquire knowledge. These four are essential elements for learning in science and design technology. Concepts and knowledge characterize a scientific and technological way of looking at the world, whilst the skills, or ways of working, are essential in developing, testing and using such concepts and knowledge. The development of certain personal qualities promote pupil involvement, encourage learning and enhance the quality of the work in science and design technology. These main objectives are represented diagrammatically in Figure 2.1. In working towards them it is important that the lines of investigation which the children pursue are matched as closely as possible to their developmental stage and individual needs.

It is perhaps worth noting here that the development of personal qualities and skills are largely 'content free', that is they can be developed irrespective of the subject matter. The development of concepts and knowledge, however, tend to be more 'content specific' and teachers need to be aware of this when considering balance in implementing the National Curriculum. Of importance also, in selecting topics for study, is the realization that understanding of particular concepts can be developed through quite different content with the acquisition of a different body of knowledge. For example, the concept of environment can be developed through the study of the school pond, a sea-shore, a local wood, the school itself or the local shops, the knowledge acquired in each case being totally different.

In the case of Gavin and his peers, they were developing an understanding of a number of ideas or concepts such as that of an insect being an animal with six legs which has a body consisting of three parts, a head, thorax and abdomen. They were also developing the concept of life cycle, that is, an adult producing an egg which subsequently grows into another adult of the same kind, together with the concept of growth. At the same time, Gavin was also developing the concepts of cause and effect in testing his light bulbs, of environment in designing his locust cage and of cost effectiveness in making it. The particular knowledge he acquired concerned the making of an electrical circuit, to heat and light the locust cage, and insects, since he compared the similarities and differences between stick insects and locusts. The work also allowed him to develop certain personal qualities such as working effectively alongside his peers, developing a respect for living things like insects and a growing aesthetic awareness in designing the locust cage. With regard to skills, amongst others, he was involved in developing manipulative skills, investigative skills and those concerned with designing and making.

Science and Design Technology: Similarities and Differences

All that has been said so far refers to both science and design technology education and, in the primary context, it is right that both are viewed holistically within the curriculum. However, it is of concern that teachers are aware of the similarities and differences between the two and, most importantly, come to realize that technological capability can be developed through many areas of the curriculum such as home economics, business studies

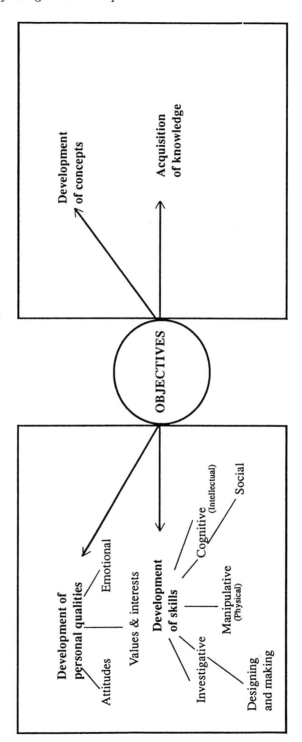

Figure 2.1: Classification of Educational Objectives

(economic awareness), craft, design and technology, the creative arts, information technology, mathematics, health education, and the humanities.

A study of both science and design technology involves solving problems but those that are technological usually arise as the result of a human need: in the case of Gavin, the need to provide an appropriate home for locusts. The solution to the technological problem is a practical one which almost invariably involves the designing and making of an artefact, system or environment (the locust cage), which is tested to see if it meets requirements. In Gavin's case it was necessary to maintain a fixed temperature through the use of a light bulb to produce heat. This involved the wiring of a circuit and the selection of an appropriate light bulb for the size of the cage. Adequate aeration and space for the animals also had to be taken into consideration together with a mechanism for feeding and cleaning out, the cost of materials and the quality and aesthetic nature of the finished product. A solution was found which best met the requirements within the limits of the problem, the cost and Gavin's capabilities. On the other hand, the scientific problem which Gavin was involved in, that of investigating the food preferences of stick insects, was concerned more with discovery than invention (as in the case of the locust cage) and research for its own sake. A conclusion, rather than an artefact was required as an end point and few constraints (such as cost, utility and aesthetically pleasing nature of the finished product) needed to be taken into account in solving the problem.

However, in solving both scientific and technological problems it is necessary not only to develop an understanding of concepts and acquire knowledge but also to promote the application of previous learning in new situations. The development of certain personal qualities and social skills, such as the ability to work in groups, are also important to both areas of the curriculum. Perhaps the most striking similarity between science and design technology education is in the 'process' or investigative skills employed. The skills which Gavin used in investigating food preference of stick insects were precisely the same as those used in testing the locust cage. To obtain a valid answer in the first problem Gavin set up a situation whereby he presented, in the same container, two green and two yellow similar sized sprays of privet to four stick insects. In order to measure the amount of food eaten, he first outlined each leaf on graph paper so that he could compare the area at a later date. Figure 2.2 is a record of his work. He had controlled, or kept the same, the variables of container size, number of stick insects and food quantity so that he could investigate, by changing only the type of privet, whether the kind of food made a difference to the quantity eaten. Similarly, in testing the locust cage for its ability to maintain a specific temperature, he investigated different light bulbs changing only one thing at a time, the wattage, to see if wattage made a difference to the temperature maintained.

Matching, Continuity and Progression

So far it has been the intention to give a broad overview of science and design technology education. Using Gavin as a case study it has been possible to see how, as well as developing certain personal qualities, he has been involved in first-hand practical experiences which helped him develop certain concepts (acquiring the associated knowledge at the same time) and skills. In practical terms, however, how might similar learning opportunities be provided for children of different ages and abilities? How can we provide a curriculum which is differentiated sufficiently to take into account the various

Figure 2.2: Food Preferences of Stick Insects

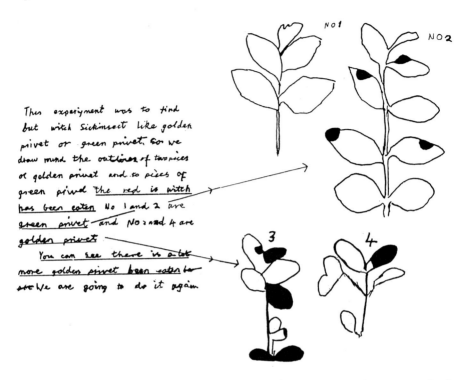

This experiment was to find
but witch Sickinsect like golden
privet or green privet, so we
draw round the outlines of two pieces
of golden privet and so pieces of
green privet the red is witch
has been eaten No 1 and 2 are
green privet and No 3 and 4 are
golden privet
You can see there is a lot
more golden privet been eaten so
etc We are going to do it again

stages of development of children and which allows for continuity and progression both within and between schools?

Learning in science and design technology primarily involves the development of skills and understanding of concepts and, although at first children's thoughts may be rudimentary, they develop gradually through encouragement and experience. However, development is not readily described in simple terms, and the change from less mature to more mature states includes several strands. The two most important strands are the change in nature of the skill or concept and the change in the kinds of situations in which they can be successfully deployed. For progress to take place it is important that children are involved in activities which 'match' their level of development. In some cases a greater variety of experience at the same level is what is required while in others, the child may be ready to take a small step forward and the level of activity provided must reflect this. This idea, however, pre-supposes a knowledge and understanding of the developmental progression expected in most children and an ability, on the part of the teacher, to identify the point along it which individuals have reached. In developing this notion further, it will be clearer if the development of skills and concepts are considered separately.

Skills

Pupils need to be exposed from an early age to the investigative skills of problem solving and testing, that is, observing, raising questions, communicating, measuring, predicting, interpreting data and hypothesizing. Following a topic on toys, children at an early stage of development when asked of a mixed bag of balls, 'which is the best bouncer?' may merely empty them upon the floor and engage in free play! Later on, they will be able to discuss, possibly with their teacher, what is meant by 'best'. Does it mean bounce the highest, for the longest time, the furthest or the greatest number of bounces? When they are ready to try to find out which one bounces the highest, for example, they may begin by predicting and then testing one ball against another or all the balls separately, using a child or a mark on the wall as a guide to height, as in Figure 2.3. It is likely, at this stage, that they do not see the need to control any of the variables involved, least of all the height from which the ball is originally dropped! At a later stage they will be ready to make the test 'fair' by controlling the single variable of height but ignoring others that are relevant to the investigation. A more sophisticated record made by children at this stage of development is shown in Figure 2.4. Later, children will control other variables such as the way in which the ball is dropped, the person who records the height of bounce or the surface upon which the bounce takes place. For children who are more advanced in their thinking, the more difficult problem of finding out whether the best bouncer in one context is also the best in another might be posed. Figure 2.5 is a record of the work of a group of children who compared the results of bouncing balls on different surfaces. The National Curriculum Attainment Target 1, Exploration of Science, is concerned with this aspect of Science Education (DES, 1989c).

Pupils should develop the intellectual and practical skills that allow them to explore the world of science and develop a further understanding of scientific phenomena and the procedure of scientific exploration and investigation. This

Figure 2.3: Using Edward to See How High the Balls Bounced

Figure 2.4: A Representational Graph to Show How High the Balls Bounced

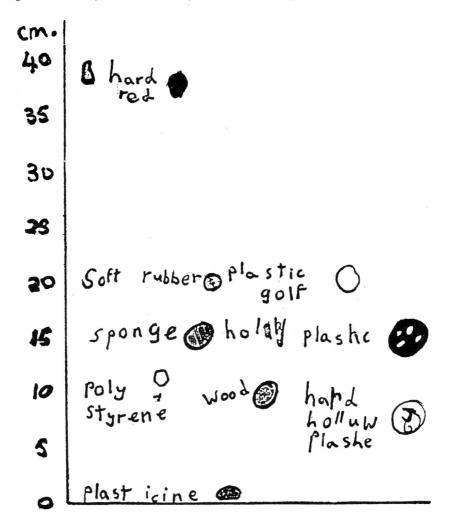

work should take place in the context of activities that require a progressively more systematic and quantified approach, which draws upon an increasing knowledge and understanding of science. The activities should encourage the ability to:

    i. plan, hypothesise and predict.
   ii. design and carry out investigations.
  iii. interpret results and findings.
  iv. draw inferences.
   v. communicate exploratory tasks and experiments.

The statements of attainment for each level provide guidance with respect to the development of such skills (see Figure 2.6).

Figure 2.5: A Record of How High Balls Bounced on Different Surfaces

No	Bounce height		
	carpet	polystyrene	card
1	No bounce	200mm	No bounce
2	140mm	240mm	110mm
3	190mm	290mm	80mm
4	250mm	170mm	270mm
5	320mm	40mm	110mm
6	730mm	310mm	380mm
7	300mm	220mm	280mm
8	300mm	290mm	390mm
9	530mm	500mm	460mm
10	500mm	380mm	430mm
11	520mm	400mm	290mm
12	430mm	360mm	390mm
13	290mm	200mm	240mm
14	150mm	470mm	170mm
Averages	**331**	**291**	**258**

Figure 2.6: Attainment target 1: Exploration of science

Exploration of science, communication, and the application of knowledge and understanding (AT1)

Level Statements of attainment

Pupils should:

1
- observe familiar materials and events in their immediate environment, at first hand, using their senses.
- describe and communicate their observations, ideally through talking in groups or by other means, within their class.

2
- ask questions and suggest ideas of the 'how', 'why', and 'what will happen if' variety.
- identify simple differences, for example, *hot/cold, rough/smooth.*
- use non-standard and standard measures, for example, *hand-spans and rulers.*
- list and collate observations.
- interpret findings by associating one factor with another, for example, *the pupils' perception at this level that 'light objects float', 'thin wood is bendy'.*
- record findings in charts, drawings and other appropriate forms.

3
- formulate hypotheses, for example, *'this ball will bounce higher than that one'.*
- identify, and describe simple variables that change over time, for example, *growth of a plant.*
- distinguish between a 'fair' and 'unfair' test.
- select and use simple instruments to enhance observations, for example, *a stop-clock or hand lens.*
- quantify variables, as appropriate, to the nearest labelled division of simple measuring instruments, for example, *a rule.*
- record experimental findings, for example, *in tables and bar charts.*
- interpret simple pictograms and bar charts.
- interpret observations in terms of a generalized statement, for example, *the greater the suspended weight, the longer the spring.*
- describe activities carried out by sequencing the major features.

4
- raise questions in a form which can be investigated.
- formulate testable hypotheses.
- construct 'fair tests'.
- plan an investigation where the plan indicates that the relevant variables have been identified and others controlled.
- select and use a range of measuring instruments, as appropriate, to quantify observations of physical quantities, such as volume and temperature.
- follow written instructions and diagrammatic representations.
- carry out an investigation with due regard to safety.
- record results by appropriate means, such as the construction of simple tables, bar charts, line graphs.
- draw conclusions from experimental results.
- describe investigations in the form of ordered prose, using a limited technical vocabulary.

5
- use concepts, knowledge and skills to suggest simple questions and design investigations to answer them.
- identify and manipulate relevant independent and dependent variables, choosing appropriately between ranges, numbers and values.
- select and use measuring instruments to quantify variables and use more complex measuring instruments with the required degree of accuracy, for example, *minor divisions on thermometers and forcemeters.*
- make written statements of the patterns derived from the data obtained from various sources.

In design technology, as well as developing the investigative skills necessary to test the artefacts, systems or environments which have been produced, a progression can also be expected in the type of materials used, the knowledge and past experience required to make them operative, the degree of sophistication exhibited in the finished product and the context within which it was produced.

Continuing with the toys topic, it might be useful to consider, at this point, the kind of activities which might be provided for children who are at various stages in the development of technological and investigative skills and who all want to work with spinning tops. Figure 2.6 shows the expected progression of investigative skills from levels one to four as stated in the document 'Science in the National Curriculum'.

At Level 1, children might collect a variety of toy spinning tops and try them out to find out which was the best. This would stimulate a considerable amount of discussion about what is meant by 'best' and both observational and communication skills would be developed.

At Level 2, children might make their own tops using card and a pencil as a spindle. Performance could be compared and the findings interpreted, e.g. large tops are best and so on.

At Level 3, performance of the tops could be timed with a stopclock. By constructing 'fair tests' simple variables such as disc material or size could be investigated and findings recorded and interpreted in terms of appropriate material and size of disc.

At Level 4, a variety of variables could be investigated such as disc material, disc size, length of spindle, position of disc, spinning surface and so on. The level of sophistication of this kind of activity would require an ability, amongst others, to 'fair test' and thus control variables, formulate testable hypotheses and draw conclusions.

In terms of the development of technological skills, the spinning top activity has much potential.

In working towards Attainment Target 1 (see *Design and Technology for Ages 5–16*), children would identify the need for a better spinning top and would be given the opportunity to design and make one. In producing a realistic design, they would be working towards Attainment Target 2 and in planning and making their tops, they would be working towards Attainment Target 3. Attainment Target 4, Evaluation, links particularly with the testing of the various kinds of tops.

Concepts

Conceptual understanding and the acquisition of knowledge also progresses as children develop; this is reflected in the Statements of Attainment in the Science Knowledge and Understanding Profile Component. For example, in Attainment Target 3 Processes of Life, the expected progression in the understanding of the human life cycle, is stated as follows:

Level 2 Know that living things reproduce their own kind.
Level 3 Be able to describe the main stages in the human life cycle.

Level 4 Understand the process of reproduction in mammals.

Level 5 Know living things are made up from different kinds of cells which carry out different jobs.

Level 6 Understand the processes of conception in human beings.

This example has been chosen particularly because it is one of the few areas which have to rely on second-hand sources (video, slide/tape sequences, charts and books) for its delivery. Similar progressions can be highlighted in other Attainment Targets, but development in understanding is expected to be achieved through first-hand experience of practical activities. In the primary phase, 45 to 50 per cent of curriculum time is expected to be spent on Attainment Target 1, the Exploration of Science, that is, on activities of a problem solving nature. However, the 'content' upon which they are based must come from the thirteen Attainment Targets in Profile Component 2, Knowledge and Understanding of Science. In this way, the development of skills and conceptual understanding can progress side by side.

For example, in Attainment Target 6, at Level 4, children should be 'developing the ability to be able to make comparisons between materials on the basis of simple properties of strength or hardness'. They will also be learning 'to relate knowledge of these properties to the everyday use of materials', that is, develop the concept of property related to function or use. An activity which could be used to work towards these Statements of Attainment might be to design, make and test a shopping bag. In this context it would be necessary to try out a variety of materials and bag designs. This would involve not only working towards Science Attainment Target 1 in 'planning an investigation where the plan indicates that the relevant variables have been identified and others controlled', but also working towards all four of the Attainment Targets identified in the document *Design and Technology for Ages 5–16*.

A final point to make here is that the ability to solve problems and design and make artefacts, systems or environments also depends greatly upon the level of conceptual understanding of the key areas involved, and thus, in designing the curriculum, it is crucial that an appropriate balance is obtained between the main conceptual areas.

The Way Forward

By what has been said above, it is obvious that science and design technology education should involve children, for the most part, in first-hand experience of practical problem solving activities. In this way, opportunity is provided for them to progress in their thinking allowing them to develop further skills and concepts within the context of the natural and man-made world.

A number of teachers have already moved towards this way of working by developing a closer understanding of the nature of science and design technology and adopting a more appropriate range of resources and teaching styles to implement it. However, many still need to make this step. Chapter 3 attempts to identify what needs to be achieved in the long term and provides some pointers as to how this might be done.

Chapter 3

What Changes Need to Be Achieved?

Introduction

The emphasis given in chapter 2 to a problem solving view of science and design technology is one which is gaining greater credibility among teachers. A number of teachers in the primary phase have already moved a long way towards an experiential approach to learning, strengthened by a sound progression of the processes and conceptual progression involved in science and design technology education. This change has been achieved by teachers involving themselves in INSET activities and, subsequently, systematically acquiring and adopting a wide range of teaching styles. Gradually, by the provision of an enriched learning environment, schools have learned to provide a greater range of resources which are linked more clearly to the needs of a differentiated curriculum.

If such a curriculum is to be available permanently to all children within a school, then at an early stage it is helpful if a statement of policy is committed to paper. Initially the policy may be expressed in outline terms which will suffice to help all the teachers in the school move towards the situation described above.

In implementing such a policy, it has been realized that appropriate learning activities can best be provided after a careful assessment of pupil performance has been carried out. Indeed, much of the development which has taken place in Bedfordshire schools in this area over the past decade is now supported and reinforced by the requirements of the National Curriculum, which provides a sound framework for the changes described in this chapter to take place. Inevitably such changes, if they become permanently implemented, will affect the approaches to teaching and learning of the pupils at the next and subsequent stages.

Understanding the Nature of Science and Design Technology

Clearly an understanding of the skills and concepts involved in science and design technology is essential. So too is the ability to assess, with some accuracy, the point to which children have progressed. If teachers are to provide a science and design technology entitlement curriculum for all pupils, then they will need quickly to come to terms with these two statements. Considerable time and energy will need to be spent on teachers' own conceptual understanding of the Attainment Targets in the National Curriculum (DES, 1989c) in order that they are aware of the stages through which children progress in their learning. The same applies to the acquisition of skills. Only then will teachers be in a position to match activities to the stages of development of individual children. Many good teachers of younger children operate in this manner intuitively. The National Curriculum will, however, demand a similar response from all teachers if they are to take an objective approach to the assessment of progress in learning in science and design technology.

The National Curriculum Science Profile Component 1, 'Exploration of Science', is concerned with the acquisition of skills and, as pointed out in chapter 2, is 'content free'. It is expected that although, in the primary phase, about half the curriculum time for science should be devoted to this component, the content upon which it is based should be drawn from Profile Component 2 'Knowledge and Understanding in Science'. This is directly in line with the objectives for science and design technology put forward in Figure 2.1 in chapter 2 and does not conflict in any way with the philosophy for science and design technology education which has been promulgated over the last decade.

However, although it is accepted that problem solving activities have taken their place in the curriculum of most primary schools, now that programmes of study have been laid down for each of the key stages, it will mean that schools may need to broaden the content upon which such activities are based. For example, have Forces (AT.10), Electricity and Magnetism (AT.11), Energy (AT.13), Human Influences upon the Earth (AT.5) and Microelectronics (AT.12) always been regularly included as a basis for childrens' activities? Are opportunities for design technology (AT. 1–4) always provided?

With regard to assuring children's abilities with a view to matching and offering differentiated curriculum, teachers will need to take into account the statements of attainment for each of the relevant Attainment Targets. Implicit in this is the need to understand what each of the statements mean and, for some teachers, this will involve coming to terms with new conceptual areas. A great many teachers will need to pursue their understanding to greater depths if they are to help children progress. This may mean the provision, on the part of the LEA, of the resources necessary to allow for such INSET opportunities.

Before any real progress can be made, teachers need the opportunity to try out, at their own level, investigations which might be carried out by their own pupils. By so doing, teachers begin to understand more quickly the value of first-hand experience in acquiring real insight into either the problems involved in a task or the progressive development of concepts. Having experienced this process for themselves, when they set similar tasks for their own pupils, they learn to resist the temptation to intervene and spend their time making observations of pupils, from which they are more likely to begin to understand how children learn. It is only then that they are in a position to understand how carefully investigative experiences must be designed. When a teacher begins to fully understand this process and provide adequately for it to happen on a regular basis, a beginning has been made in understanding the value of a practical approach.

Adopting a Range of Appropriate Teaching Styles

Experiential learning means that teachers will need to play the role of resource manager by providing ideas, resources and access to information which is appropriate to their particular needs at the time. Very quickly, after teachers have come to terms with the provision of an activity based science and design technology curriculum, they realize that the way in which they organize their classroom becomes a key issue.

Instinctively the lively teacher will be aware of the need to manage the complexities of the classroom situation. With a great deal of thought and care, from time to time, it will almost certainly be necessary for the whole or part of the classroom to be changed around to accommodate an activity. In the case of younger children, the re-organization of a classroom will always be the responsibility of the teacher. With older pupils, who are used to working in this way, they will almost certainly make suggestions and will be willing to rearrange the classroom if necessary. The creative management of the total resource available to promote learning becomes a crucial role for the teacher to play.

Having arrived at this position and perhaps experimented with different forms of organization they also realize the effect which this has on their approach to the provision of activity-based learning. Additionally, experiments of this kind are the easiest way in which teachers realize the need for a whole variety of teaching styles and forms of organization necessary in order to maximize the opportunities for learning in an increasingly technology based society.

The implementation of a science and design technology curriculum necessitates a recognition by the teacher that the task can only effectively be addressed by adopting a number of different roles and requiring different expectations of individual children. Some of the roles are easily recognized, for example, when the teacher acts as an instructor. Occasionally a particular activity may demand clear and precise guidance before pupils are allowed to proceed. In some instances the teacher may need to ensure that all safety precautions have been taken before the pupils make a start. Other roles may be less familiar to the majority but none the less important in the delivery of well differentiated curricular experiences for children. A good teacher will always be on the lookout for new and interesting materials through which new concepts and skills may be developed and knowledge and understanding may be acquired. Such a role might be described as provider of resource items. Inextricably linked to this role are the teachers' expectations of their pupils. With the right level of expectation applied to the group, pupils will always respond and reward teachers in ways which exceed their original expectations. The various desirable attributes associated with the learning of science and design technology can only be developed by providing pupils with opportunity backed by expectation.

Having made appropriate resource provision, the teacher will want to facilitate an activity which might also be the subject of negotiation with an individual or group of pupils. This role will take on new dimensions as the learning and understanding of children grows. The level of questioning by both pupils and teacher should reveal the stage which has been reached. Thus acting as facilitator, the teacher is providing the pupils with the best opportunity to react to a situation and to develop from it. Children who are secure in an environment with the teacher playing a different role, are more likely to develop ideas without the notion that their answers must always be 'correct'. Such a situation is healthy and more likely to lead to the development of true learning and understanding. Teachers involved with children in this way have always developed a sensitivity about the most appropriate time to intervene; the wrong intervention may destroy an important concept forever in a childs mind whilst an intervention at the right time may help children progress in their thinking.

As the group of pupils progressively develop their understanding of the world around them and increase in their autonomy and confidence, they will benefit considerably from the opportunity to organize their own learning. This might well mean organizing themselves or learning to work as a group or team. It is more likely to happen if they gradually become responsible for resourcing their ideas by organizing the materials and equipment to carry out the research necessary to develop an idea; then individual learning curves in science and design technology will become steeper.

When experience and knowledge has reached the stage which will allow individual or group hypothesizing to take place on a regular basis, challenges (increasing in difficulty and needing much thought and research on behalf of the individual in formulating a hypothesis) will need to be provided and the outcomes assessed accurately. At about this stage it will be necessary for some of the interests and abilities of pupils to be fitted in to a slightly more structured approach.

The notion of 'structure' is difficult to grasp as it is set against a background of a complex situation, the classroom, and is affected by extremely subtle and sensitive pressures exerted through the interaction of those involved, their relationship to one another and with the learning environment. Structuring the learning environment is important. The idea or topic through which learning is organized, the provision of appropriate resource materials and the reporting of the outcomes in acceptable ways, allows children to develop at their own rate.

More important still, as far as the teacher is concerned, is to know with some degree of certainty that learning is taking place. For each child to progress in the acquisition of knowledge and understanding and apply their learning to new situations, the teacher must be aware of the level at which the children are currently working. Knowledge of the operational level of individual children is acquired by teachers observing children, over a long period of time, working at a number of tasks designed to promote learning. Familiarity with the Attainment Targets of the National Curriculum will provide a framework within which this can happen. As facilitators, teachers should constantly be asking themselves the questions, 'Am I certain about the level which an individual child has reached?' 'How can I build on this and provide for the next activity so that more progress can be made?' All this 'structure' has to be fitted into the context of the community, the school and the demands placed upon teachers in the management of a busy classroom situation.

In contemporary terms, the National Curriculum can provide a useful framework to structure the science and design technology curriculum, but it leaves teachers to apply their professional judgment about the progress being made and the way in which it is reported (DES, 1989a, 1989c). By sharing experiences, the staff can develop their response to the demands of the teaching and learning situation. Through formal or informal discussion of classroom activity, teachers can share a developing understanding of the needs of their pupils. This kind of discussion can be enhanced considerably by a programme of observing each other at work in the classroom or by observing children at work in another teacher's classroom, all of which is now possible if the LEA funds for the INSET programme are devolved to support school-based initiatives. (There are many examples available by which a teacher can research what actually takes place in the classroom. A short span of well recorded classroom observation can often provide the substance of many hours of fruitful discussion amongst groups of teachers.) Discussions of this kind can have many useful outcomes, one of which might be the ways in which an individual teacher plans the use of her/his time more effectively, ultimately to the benefit of the pupils involved.

Providing for Relevance, Breadth, Balance, Continuity and Progression

Although it is accepted that learning for learning's sake is a valuable experience, it is crucial to ensure that a science and design technology curriculum is developed which is more relevant to the needs of pupils in the society in which they will live. Relevance, in this instance, refers to two aspects of need, that associated with the individual interests and experiences of the pupil and that associated with the world in which he/she lives. For example, it is important that children are aware and understand the functioning of the electronic domestic environment, but a context for study must be chosen which, in order to develop learning potential, motivates individuals. It might be preferable for one child to work on a burglar alarm system for a house and for another to design an electronically controlled gate system which allows a car to enter a garage without the driver needing to get out of the vehicle.

Moving back into the teaching and learning situation found in a typical primary classroom, it might be more relevant, say, for children who have no easy access to the sea shore, to study fresh water life in the school pond, if the focus is to be study of a biological environment. Similarly 'junk modelling' will have little or no relevance to the children involved with the activity if the models, in their view, are unable to perform the task for which they were designed. A model of a car needs to be able to move freely and be provided with a simple power source enabling it to progress along a surface. Such a power source can be as sophisticated as a motor or as simple as a twisted elastic band. In a science lesson, for example, the theory of gear systems has little relevance to children if the work is not extended into the production of working models which put theory into practice.

Alongside a relevant curriculum, children also need to be exposed to a breadth of experience; it is important that this notion is built into a statement of curriculum policy. A wide range of experiences in any one area will provide children with the foundations on which they can build at a later stage. An enormous range of experiences will almost certainly be provided by an experienced teacher of younger children and these need to be fitted in to a more structured framework as the children progress.

The National Curriculum now provides us with guidelines for achieving this through the Programmes of Study. It has already been mentioned earlier in this chapter that, certain areas of experience such as energy, forces and electronics have traditionally been neglected. Now under the Statutory Orders, it will no longer be possible to let this happen. In addition, children will need to be given far greater opportunity to solve problems concerned with a wider range of phenomena in the world around them. When new topics for study are selected and planning begins, issues of this kind become crucial if the continuity of curricular experience is to be maintained.

The provision of a balanced curriculum is also important in terms of providing children with a framework upon which to build. Currently, consideration will need to be given to the requirements of the National Curriculum for science in terms of the weighting given to each profile component and, within these, individual attainment targets. The notion of weighting is significant because it is not only concerned with the summative assessment of individual children, but also, more importantly, should reflect the curriculum time allocated. A balance must be struck which gives a fair allocation of time to practical activity alongside and in conjunction with the development of knowledge and understanding. Within this component certain attainment targets may need to be given greater prominence than others.

All of this has considerable significance when the balance of science and design technology and the place of these subjects in the total curriculum is considered. In practice, the question of the total curriculum balances must be discussed by the staff of a school at the earliest stages, when they are planning a new project or topic together. Each topic will need to be examined not only in terms of the science and design technology Attainment Targets included within it, but also with respect to other curriculum areas, particularly in English and mathematics. The implications of the time allocated to English, maths, science and design technology within each topic will need careful consideration and a mechanism for this examination must be found quickly by schools. Much of the practice in the primary phase recognizes the value of integration within the curriculum. The overwhelming problem which faces teachers now is the increased need to integrate 'subjects' within topic work since curriculum time will be at a premium if all the Attainment Targets in the National Curriculum are to be met over a period of time.

The content of a topic which may either relate to one class or provide experience for all pupils in a school, will now need to be analyzed in terms of curricular provision over a longer time scale. For example, are all the Attainment Targets being covered? Does the weighting given to the individual Attainment Targets within Science Profile component 2 determine the curriculum 'time' allocated to them? Similarly the balance between Science Profile Components 1 and 2 must be taken into account in the planning and subsequent implementation. Do proposed technological activities always work towards the achievement of all four Attainment Targets? Is the work carried out in a wide range of contexts where this is appropriate? Attention will also need to be given to the establishment of a proper balance between the knowledge and skills upon which the activities are based and the opportunity to consider values. Once more agreements made between the staff of a school concerning balance need to be clearly expressed in a policy statement.

This point is important when considering continuity and progression. Autonomy is a valued attribute among teachers; it is also a quality displayed by pupils, particularly when they are asked to participate in an activity such as a simulation which allows them to exhibit their personal qualities. Once again the teacher must carefully balance the opportunity which is given to pupils to develop ideas and their thinking against their own experience and to ensure that skill development, concepts, knowledge, attitudes and values are progressively acquired. Any teachers working to their maximum potential will find such a balance difficult to achieve in reality. The classroom situation is an extremely complex place of work. Among any group of pupils is a gradient of experience, maturity and ability which can only be adequately developed by providing a rich range of learning experiences which are carefully assessed on an individual basis through observation. Only when this has been done can the teacher hope to provide learning experiences which match the abilities of individuals. One further reason why planning the matching experience to activity is of major importance is the issue of continuity of experience for individual pupils. All teachers can now work from the same base-line, the National Curriculum. It is important, therefore, that the work of one teacher complements the work of another.

The Statements of Attainment, for each of the Attainment Targets, offer excellent guidance here, provided that the activities in which the children take part allow the particular criterion statement to be applied. For example, (Science Attainment Target 15) it is obvious that it will not be possible to ascertain whether a pupil knows that light can be made to change direction, indicating that he or she is operating at level 3, if he or she has not been given the opportunity to work with mirrors and a light source. The value of the Statements of Attainment is therefore threefold. They not only provide an indication of what children should be involved in and might be achieving, but also disclose the level at which they are currently working. They thus provide an excellent diagnostic tool for analyzing curricular provision, for the achievement of matching and helping children progress, and for ensuring that continuity of experience is achieved.

If the Statements of Attainment are to be used to best effect, teachers will need to be assessing their pupils as part of an ongoing process. This formative evaluation using the criteria embodied in the various Statements of Attainment, implies the use of a wide range of classroom observational techniques. These might include questioning, dialogue, listening, watching children work and appraising children's work records. An excellent account of this way of working is to be found in the materials of *Match and Mismatch*.

An important point to make here is that this is only an extension of what many teachers have already been doing. The need carefully and continuously to assess pupil performance (formative assessment), is now a paramount requirement of all teachers. In the past, statements of formative assessment have often been made of pupils by teachers on an occasion such as a parents' evening. Continuous formative assessment of pupil progress will not only now be required on those formal occasions, but will need to be made and recorded occasionally throughout the school year! Systems for recording formative observations of progress will need to be agreed upon and implemented. It should be further stressed that formative assessment is for the purpose of providing continuity of experience and, therefore, helping children to progress in their learning, rather than labelling them at an early stage.

Coming to Terms With Summative Assessment

The demands of the National Curriculum require that all children are assessed at each of the four key stages. Appropriately, for each Attainment Target, a large proportion of the final outcome will be based upon the teacher's own assessment of individual children and this summative assessment in turn, will be based on the formative assessment described above.

However, from now on, not only will the teacher be required to record progress through observation, it will also be necessary to devise practical tasks similar to those being developed nationally for this purpose, for pupils to perform as an ongoing requirement. In connection with this, teachers may need to devise their own criteria by which they can assess whether particular statements of attainment have been reached. An agreed system of recording their observations will also be essential.

The validity of assessment of pupil performance is so important that it should be enshrined in policy at a very early stage. Continuity of experience for the pupils is crucial, together with the creation of a physical and intellectual environment which allows individuals to progress in their thinking at their own rate. Severe disruption of this continuity of experience occurs when it is not fully recognized that considerable discussion on this issue needs to take place both within and between schools. Therefore, the initial statement of policy will need to recognize the crucial discussion stage which later, when formulated more fully, becomes part of the substantive statement of policy.

Rethinking Resource Provision

The demands of the National Curriculum in both science and design technology will require schools and LEAs to review the basic materials and equipment required to implement it. This has been brought about not only in relation to the increased numbers of children who will be involved in scientific and technological activity at any one time (due to the increased curricular time required) but also by the nature of the activities involved and their level of sophistication.

For example in Key Stage 1, children will be required to use a wide range of measuring instruments. This will involve schools purchasing 'thermostiks' for measuring temperature and newton meters for measuring force, in addition to the more conventional measuring instruments. In Key Stage 2, a wide range of electronic equipment will be needed for data handling, data collection and control technology. Throughout the Primary Phase, a comprehensive range of tools and materials will be required if children are to achieve technological capability. It would seem that this matter can only be addressed effectively as part of a rolling programme for development both within the school and the LEA.

The Formulation of a Policy for Change

Schools will be in various stages of development with regard to the changes described above and it would be foolish to contemplate implementation all at once. What is important, however, is that a policy for change is formulated and a plan for its implementation is constructed with a realistic time scale in mind. The provision by all schools of a National Curriculum Development Plan is now a statutory requirement.

Finally the issue of evaluation in terms of what needs to be achieved must be addressed. A dynamic approach to teaching and learning can only effectively be achieved if an evaluation element is built into the earlier stages of policy formulation. Evaluation strategies need to be considered in a number of ways; from the simple short term evaluation of a classroom project, to the more sophisticated long term review of how curriculum change affects the whole school. Consideration of this major issue needs to be firmly addressed when designing the National Curriculum Development Plan for the school.

Chapter 4

Formulating a Policy for Change

Introduction

Any change necessitates all those involved in learning to do something new. It is important to recognize that this is as applicable to LEAs as it is to schools or individuals. Of equal importance is the need to be quite clear about what it is that needs to be changed and what it needs to be changed to, what needs to be accomplished and how.

Central to any change process must be the fundamental consideration of the needs of children. Realization that all children learn in different ways, have different interests and motivations is at last being reflected in the provisions made by primary teachers. In the primary school consisting of, say, twelve teachers, including the head, it is more than usual these days to find two or three teachers, plus the head and deputy, who might recognize the need for change and between them have the energy and ability to carry the process through to some kind of conclusion.

In the not too distant past, the in-service course provision for teachers interested in the teaching of science to younger children was clearly not achieving the desired effect of delivering science in the classroom. In some instances attempts were made to convert them into science teachers as a result of attending a six week course consisting of a couple of hours per week after school. Another way tried was to provide equipment which was thought to be scientific, in some cases this was used with enthusiasm but mostly it was quickly assigned to the 'science-cupboard' with a few other unlikely bits and pieces of rubbish. Any inspector will be only too familiar with the sights revealed by opening such a cupboard! Clearly a new way had to be found.

It was only after many failures to interest primary teachers in the excitment which could be achieved through successful science teaching, that work began in earnest to develop a method of applying the limited resources available to find a solution which would really work. The first priority was to seek out situations where there was a willingness for change to be accepted. Eventually, to cut a very long story short, it was found that a combination of scientific experience and curriculum change theory, applied with some energy, was to succeed. Those familiar with the application of the change process to other areas of the curriculum may have already noticed that the general principles associated with change can be applied equally well to any area of the curriculum.

Past experience has shown that those schools who wanted to take on developments in science did so by going for an interpretation of the 'subject' for younger children. For the most part this consisted of an application of the content of the secondary science curriculum in sufficient detail to satisfy the curiosity of the pupils they taught. In-service courses, too, were designed largely to improve teachers' ability in the subject and not necessarily their knowledge of how younger children acquire their understanding of science. This may be precisely why in the 1960s and 70s the teaching of scientific understanding to young children largely failed despite the valiant attempts of the Schools Council, the Nuffield Foundation and many others to help promote the place of science within this age group.

It was a rarity during those two decades, to find a primary teacher who fully understood the scientific learning needs of younger children. Occasionally such a teacher could be found who was having a real effect on children's ability in science. Such a find was a rare oasis in the dry desert of scientific learning. If this teacher happened to be a class teacher in a junior school, then possibly only the pupils in that particular class would reap the benefit. Even fewer positive attempts to teach science could be found in infant schools; such a find was even rarer. Work in design and technology was largely absent at this time.

The Need for a Policy for Change

At school level there is no doubt that what needs to be achieved in every classroom is a teaching style which provides for children being educated through first-hand experience. However, this alone is not enough; teachers need be able to distinguish between activities which merely provide children with something to do and those which provide them with an educational experience. This implies that the teacher must have an understanding of the processes involved, backed by a knowledge of a wide range of appropriate activities, be able to match activities to individuals and have the ability to provide for continuity and progression. Furthermore, it is necessary to provide for breadth, balance and relevance when integrating the work within the whole curriculum. Clearly, it is no longer good enough to expect this to take place by adopting an ad hoc approach. In order to achieve the situation outlined above, planning must take place so that each school adopts a school-wide policy for change set against a time scale. This idea has already been discussed in the previous chapter and is explored further in chapter 6. The requirement of the National Curriculum for each school to produce a Development Plan should help all primary schools to make progress in their thinking about the implementation of scientific and technological experiences for younger children.

The formulation of curriculum policy, is not a new phenomenon in schools. What can be attributed to the development of education in the 1980s perhaps, is the requirement for statements about policy to be written down and, what is more, the requirement for those statements to be arrived at collaboratively. For some time now it has not been possible for the headteacher to make policy statements, verbal or written, without a great deal of discussion with the staff, the parents, the governors and maybe the LEA. The new way of working in the 1990s is for schools to formulate a policy for change which allows a curriculum to be developed within the framework defined by statutory orders made by Parliament.

At LEA level, a policy for change is no less important. Of immediate concern is the recognition that every school is capable of some change provided that all staff are invited to be involved and a whole school focus is adopted. Second, it must be understood that a greater chance of success is likely to be achieved if the process involves collaboration. The implication here is that not only the school, but also the LEA, has to work quite hard in reconceptualizing the form that such external collaborative support takes. This step is crucial if such a symbiotic relationship is to be valued by both sides. Furthermore, work with individual schools needs to be carried out within a county-wide framework for school improvement if real success is to be effected overall. It is the formulation of a county-wide policy for change and the creation of a strategy for its implementation that needs to be achieved within an LEA. Planning for this process needs to be accomplished at local authority level. Those LEAs fortunate enough to have been able to take advantage of Educational Support Grants to make appointments centrally for the development of science and design technology, have achieved a great deal and have enhanced the rate of development of these two important subject areas.

The School as the Prime Unit of Change

The other significant factor aids development was the realization that the school as a whole must be considered the prime unit of change. In the early days when a new approach to the development of the science curriculum was being tried out in schools, situations were found where there was a willingness on the part of the head and staff to participate in the process. Here the use of the mathematical term 'equation' may be helpful in securing an understanding of what actually happened in the selection of schools. On one side must be the achievement of the desired change, whilst on the other side might be factors like the headteacher's attitude to change, the staff's willingness to participate, and maybe resources in the form of expertise and materials available. It is these factors which contribute to the 'culture' or 'climate' of the school. If it was felt that the factors on one side of the equation were conducive to change then a commitment to change in the form of a 'contract' between the school and the change agents was made. Here the use of the analogy of an 'equation' is similar to the notion of a school culture or climate and how it can also be affected by the application of a change process. Implied in the term 'equation' is the need to keep the developmental process in perspective or balance, a task usually undertaken by the headteacher. Situations were usually found where the head was prepared to exercise leadership skills, maintain the enthusiasm of the staff when needed, and, more importantly, take on the responsibility of pacing the development, which usually took a number of years before some form of effective implementation was achieved.

It is helpful if the staff as a group subscribe to the notion of the need for change, and, perhaps, one of their number willingly takes on the role of science curriculum coordinator. At this stage little more is needed to get started. Some groups, however, make the mistake of attempting to engrave a policy statement on 'tablets of stone' without trying out in the classroom the effectiveness of some of the ideas developed through discussion.

In an attempt to convey the complexities of a developmental experience such as this in writing it would be easy to give the impression that each 'contract' with a school is simple or even the same in each case. This is obviously not so as the circumstances in each school are different and almost certainly require very different approaches to change. Some interesting individual examples of the change process are quoted later on. However, the following actual example will perhaps illustrate some of the real problems and show how much time and effort is needed if they are to be satisfactorily solved. The final outcome regarding whether satisfaction has been achieved is a very difficult judgment to make; it also raises the question of who should be making that kind of evaluation.

After a number of school-based commitments had been entered into, from which much about leading such developments as external change agents was learned, a different 'twist' arose. All contracts made to date had been through the headteacher or by a school being approached by the external change agent involved. This example, however, arose as a result of two members of staff, the coordinators for science and environmental studies from a large primary school, attending a short awareness raising course on primary science run by the local college. During the course the two young teachers contributed well and as a result learned much which they wished to try out in their own school. The subsequent events which took place serve to illustrate some of the points raised above.

Before they finished their course the two teachers approached the LEA and asked whether it would be possible to set up such a school-based initiative, with a programme specifically designed to help their colleagues begin to find ways of providing a science curriculum for the children. They also made it clear that they had approached their head-teacher who was not quite so enthusiastic as they or the rest of the staff to enter into this kind of commitment. (It later transpired that the head saw the development of the science curriculum in his school very differently to that which was being put forward by the two teachers concerned.) The next stage was for the whole question of the approach and what to do about it to be discussed between the course leader and the adviser concerned. As a result, the adviser made an appointment to speak with the head about the idea, who, at the first meeting remained unconvinced of the need for such a time-consuming approach to development to take place in his school. After two more meetings had taken place, the second of which was between the head and both the people concerned with the running of the school-based course, the head reluctantly agreed that the possibility of such a school-based development should be put to the staff as a whole.

A staff meeting was arranged at which the adviser outlined the programme and method of working to all the teachers, including the two teachers who had attended the college course. Some questions were asked, but by the time the meeting was held, the staff was already unanimous in their support for such a course to take place in their school, specifically designed to fulfil their own needs.

Further meetings were necessary between the providers of the course who were also acting in the capacity of external change agents in this complicated and delicate situation. However, undeterred, they entered into a normal contract. This contract meant that all members of staff should attend all sessions, which were held after school, for one hour on six occasions, that they would invite the course leaders to see any displays of children's work arising out of the course and that any queries which arose about how to proceed in the classroom, would be referred to the course leaders. They, in return, would attempt to meet any reasonable request for additional necessary resources.

The most difficult problem in this case was convincing the head that the development would be desirable and that it should continue. In this instance, the role usually taken on by the head was abandoned for a contract between the head, the staff and the external change agent. But this was not only more complicated than normal but also more time-consuming for all those concerned. Keeping control of the pace of development and providing the necessary encouragement for the staff was left to the change agents to carry out as best they could under the circumstances. The delicacy of the position was such that no group or individual could be allowed to feel that they had been 'let down' in such a complex situation.

Positive results were achieved during the initial stages, for, after about a term, the course leaders were invited by the head, to look at displays which had been mounted as a result of each teacher attempting to provide practical investigative scientific experiences for their children. From these observations and further discussions with the staff it was possible to make the judgment that improvement had taken place in the provision of a science curriculum for the school. Further improvements were made in due course and a written policy finally formulated.

At this stage, it might be helpful to set the school described above into an outline context. It was built to a specification, typical of the time, which did not allow for easy communication, between class groups; each classroom being a separate entity opening onto a long corridor. Subsequent expansion in pupil numbers inevitably meant the provision of additional temporary classroom accommodation on the edge of the playing field. Pupils from the age range of 7–11, were drawn initially from families rehoused from the centre of an urban development.

Both the head and most of the staff had been in their posts for a long period of time prior to the attempt at curriculum development through to policy formulation. Continuity of experience, it could be argued, was provided by the number of years which the staff had been in the school, but because, by and large, the group remained uninfluenced by developments outside the school, little progression in thinking had taken place by the time the team arrived. However, it is important to note that the staff as a group related particularly well to one another, but as a consequence they had become quite isolated in their curriculum thinking to the extent that they were unaware, perhaps, of the need to seek refreshment from elsewhere.

The overwhelming influence on the school, without doubt, was the autocratic, even eccentric, management style of the headteacher, who considered his duty was to provide a 'syllabus' from which all members of staff were expected to work. Such a strong influence on the staff group may have given individuals some security in their role but also contributed to the isolation of the whole staff from developments which were forging ahead elsewhere in the county. Resourcing such a prescriptive programme had become restricted to a descriptive, didactic approach to delivery supported mainly by book material or TV programmes. Consequently, staff who were interested in a more practical approach, had only a very limited collection of resources with which to work.

Expectations of achievement in science, from both staff and parents, were at a low level and influenced mainly by traditional approaches to the teaching of these curriculum areas. This case study emphasizes that some of the qualitative internal features making up the climate and culture of the school were able to be changed initially by the concerted effort of the majority of the staff who were also able to appreciate, at a later stage, the value of involving relevant external collaborative support.

The greatest change occurred in this particular school when the existing head of long standing, decided to retire and was succeeded for a period by his deputy, who was invited to take on the role of acting head until a new appointment could be made. This single change in the leadership of the school had a great bearing on the subsequent pace of development. Ideas which were latent in the staff group were allowed to develop and flourish under the new leadership.

In addition, other changes in the form of temporary promotions among the rest of the staff group were made to enhance developments. Some staff left the school during this period and new appointments were made to fill the vacancies, some of which were effected through the Authority's scheme for the temporary redeployment of teaching staff. It can be seen quite clearly that development in a single school situation cannot take place in a vacuum. Rather, because of the time scale involved, development has to continue for the benefit of the pupils regardless of what is happening within the school at a particular moment. Thus by the staff making a determined, concerted effort it was possible, in this instance, to capitalize on the changes which were agreed. Changes in the staff of a school can make an enormous difference to any change process which is being implemented, but perhaps the greatest influence on the school in total is a change of headteacher.

In such a short description of a case study, the complexities of the inter-relationships among the staff may not always be apparent. For example, it is important to highlight the roles played by the leaders, including the existing head, in this situation. The head, however reluctant he may have appeared in the case study to allow things to happen, nevertheless, was persuaded by his deputy and coordinator to involve others external to the school. This step was the culmination of much activity and discussion among the staff, stimulated by the forethought of the two members of staff who realized that change was needed and who also had sufficient insight and courage to involve their own colleagues.

The point was eventually reached when the collaborative effort of the staff did not need to rely so heavily on the support of the external change agents; they were now able to plan their programmes of work cooperatively and see the relevant resource needs to implement such programmes successfully. The following is what was most important in arriving at this situation.

1   Acceptance by the staff of the need to discuss more widely, had changed their expectations with regard to individual teaching styles and learning outcomes.

2   In the example described above, the leadership given by the head was fortunately untypical of most situations. Normally the head takes on the responsibility for the task of overall leadership of the development. The head may choose subsequently to delegate the leadership role to another member of staff, say, a curriculum coordinator for a period of specific development to take place.

3   Leadership may also come in the form of any member of staff returning from a course and discussing with colleagues any aspect of what has been learned which might be relevant to the development in hand.

4   The willingness and tenacity of the staff as a group to participate fully in an agreed change is essential if development is to be successful. In this instance, the staff accepted the leadership provided by their colleagues.

5   It was important for the LEA to support their change agents and to provide them with sufficient time to see the development through to a logical conclusion: one which allowed the process to become self sustaining.

6   Finally, it is important to refer to the issue of the resource support made available to the school to allow them to progress. The resourcing of ideas to be implemented on a temporary or permanent basis in the classroom, should follow discussion and collective decision-making. After evaluation has been carried out and modifications made, the staff can progress to the next idea to be implemented with children.

These occurrences, which took place in one school, lasted just over two years, during which time a number of significant events happened. Early retirement was granted to the head, a number of staff went on to attend the same in-service course as the original two teachers and, no doubt, a significant number of other events took place during the period to retard development or even, at times, to prevent development from taking place.

The Value of External Collaborative Support

The role played by those from the LEA was very important in the extension of the development described above. The external change agents were able to use the valuable experience of collaborative effort acquired when working in other situations in the Authority. Part of the experience gained gave an insight into the manipulation which was necessary in order to fulfil the objectives of development. Gradually, the realization grew that the role of the external support provided could be redefined. It became clear, in this instance, that the successful management of change therefore demanded a supportive advisory rather than a more formal inspectorial role from the LEA.

Although it might seem obvious and desirable to employ expertise external to the school, if the person providing the support lacks sensitivity to the needs of the staff or applies expertise inappropriately, fear and mistrust may develop among the staff group, quickly followed by the loss of the credibility of the external change agent. It has been shown on numerous occasions that time spent discussing issues surrounding the employment of another person to help the process along is never wasted. However sensitively such a person enters a staff group, the dynamic of the group will be changed. Such a change in group dynamics will need to be positive and developmental if desirable outcomes are to be reached. The best professional expertise available must be recruited and given good support facilities, including the provision of resource items needed to try out ideas which a school has arrived at as a result of staff discussion. The provision of 'things scientific or technological' such as apparatus, equipment and materials, may well provide children with practical experiences but if their use is in isolation, with no regard to matching needs, motivation, ability levels, conceptual and skill development, the experience could well be meaningless in terms of the continuum of learning for an individual pupil. Similarly, the use of support external to the school, which could be from the local college or elsewhere must be considered very carefully.

Conversely, schools also need to be very clear about the kind of support they need at any point in time. When such assistance is requested by a school, not only should it be of a high quality but it should also be well matched to the needs of the school. This presupposes that the school is aware of its own needs. If, for example, the headteacher asks for the support of an advisory teacher without spending sufficient time analyzing the needs of the school at its particular stage of development, then the result of such an invitation could well be a disaster and once again credibility is at stake. The notion of matching provision for children in the classroom should apply equally to the matching of external support to the needs of the school. The contribution made by the external change agent might be highly significant in terms of the school, but of equal importance is the recognition of the role played by such an agent and the effect which this can have on those playing other roles within the school. The headteacher, on making contact with the agencies outside the school should have also thought about the appropriate pace of the development which may, out of necessity, as already shown, take place over a number of years.

As the formulation of policy exercise begins to roll and take shape in a school, it will become obvious that at some point it will be necessary to give consideration to the definition of roles of those involved with the change process. The idea is developed further in chapter 6. Consideration of the definition of role is made even more important if a decision is made by the school to involve any agency which is external to the school, like an advisory teacher or the local college. It is important then, that both the LEA and schools recognize the nature of the role played by the external change agents. When schools feel secure in the use of such support they are more likely to become pro-active in the use of outside assistance.

Formulating the Policy for Change

The previous example demonstrates a number of important points which illustrate the need to develop policy if school improvement is to take place. Earlier in this chapter, recognition is given to the need for the school to adopt, from the outset, a united approach towards improvement efforts. Some developers refer to the equation as being right, others to the climate or culture of the school being conducive to change. Initial judgments about whether even to embark upon the change process must take into consideration all factors which may be likely to effect change. At this stage of education it is no longer helpful to think in terms of the development of one subject area at the expense of all other areas of knowledge. For a long time now, primary teachers have successfully demonstrated that the provision of learning situations allowing for a rich variety of experiences to develop can help children succeed in and learn from a number of curriculum areas simultaneously. Once this focus is clearly established as a priority in the minds of the teachers, then it is safe to embark on the process of setting up a professional learning environment which is linked very positively with the evolution of curriculum policy in a number of areas. Experience has shown that schools able to take on a wide brief for development are most definitely on the road to a whole school improvement strategy. Formulating a policy for change in the real world of the primary school is a complex business. How then out of a very real situation does a written policy statement emerge? In the first instance a written record of the dates of meeting with brief minutes of what has been said and decided is important. Some kind of agreed framework is helpful to the group as a model for development. (Such a framework is described in detail in chapter 5.) It is only when such discussion has taken place, agreements have been made about how classroom practice can be effected and projects with pupils have been entered into on a trial basis, that the group can make real progress.

A policy for change, whether it is concerned with a school or an LEA, should include:

— Methods of analyzing needs;
— Suggestions for ways in which needs might be met;
— An implementation strategy;
— Monitoring and evaluation procedures.

Here are some of the major considerations which have to be taken into account where a policy for change is being formulated.

— The required change in teaching and learning styles necessary to improve childrens' understanding;
— The organizational changes necessary;
— Resource provision;
— The style of leadership required;
— The defining of roles which everyone involved should be playing;
— The need for and nature of external collaborative support;
— The implementation timescale.

The impetus for change must clearly come from somewhere; it may come from within the school or the LEA but increasingly it may come from sources other than these. Central and local government pressures are currently being applied to schools and LEAs in the form of policies for change; similarly, priorities are also being laid down at both levels of government. Provided that the policy for change imposed gives a guide to priorities and a framework for the change to happen, then the right to make the professional response to the needs of children is preserved. Additionally, if the relationship between the schools and the LEA is right, with the roles and expectations of each clearly perceived, then considerable desirable development will happen.

Finally, it would also be helpful to keep in mind the message of this chapter: that policy formulation must take place against the background of need and the realities of the situation which presents itself to the individuals involved. The formulation of a statement of written policy for change which fits the true needs of the situation is a complicated and difficult enough process. To implement it effectively needs considerable sensitivity and skill on the part of those involved.

Chapter 5

Implementing a Policy for Change
Within a School

Introduction

One example of change which most of the teaching population should remember, because the change did not take place so long ago, was the introduction of colour television. Sending acceptable black and white pictures through the air was an agreeable phenomenon which satisfied people for many years. The spread of black and white TV became almost universal; picture information and entertainment were transmitted and received in the most unlikely places. When, through research and development, that same information and entertainment could be transmitted and received in colour, everyone who owned a black and white TV wanted the extra dimension of moving colour pictures in the living room. More recently in schools, similar revolutionary change is taking place with the introduction of computers into the classroom.

The analogy could go on, but it has been sufficiently developed for the purposes of comparison. By applying the principle of an acceptable product being developed and improved so that it became more desirable and, by developing the commercial and manufacturing process, it was made available to a wider population. Perhaps it might be useful to see how this analogy can be applied to the complexities of implementing a policy for the improvement of the science and design technology curriculum in a school. How can a school set about the process of implementing and improving a black and white curriculum to one which gives a full colour dimension to every pupil? Easily, provided the willingness, energy, ability, leadership and access to information and resources are available at the time when they are most needed.

The Need to Understand the Change Process

It is a human characteristic that once a decision is made to change, the change must be achieved instantly or at least with the minimum passage of time; this certainly applies to the implementation of the National Curriculum! Going back to the analogy, how simple it would be to carry out effective curriculum development by changing the black and white TV for a colour set. Immediate transformations of this kind very rarely occur in curricular terms, even with the application, by law, of a National Curriculum. In what is perhaps the most human of all human institutions, a school, fundamental curriculum change can only effectively be achieved, in the first instance, by much discussion in order to clarify the value system which operates within. Eventually, though, the clarified agreements must be carried out through to action and written-up as policy if all the effort is to have a lasting effect and the change is to become implemented permanently. The significant point here is that, once changes have been implemented in the short term, the situation must not be allowed to re-freeze, leaving no traces of any progress originally made. In spite of the very short time-span given for the introduction of the National Curriculum in schools, it is important to realize that permanent change can only be achieved if those involved have 'ownership' of the new ways of working through being involved in the process of change described above. This is of much greater consequence to the school or the LEA, than the magnitude of the change itself or even the substance of the final outcome. There is one very good reason why a school undergoing such a process should accept and understand it fully. Whilst the change is taking place through discussion, and agreements are being reached, it will still be necessary for the teachers to begin to deliver the National Curriculum. Also whilst working in one way, teachers must be prepared to discuss the value of perhaps changing to a more appropriate teaching style. A very difficult and demanding process complicated more by the fact that often the changes in perception are small or subtle, or both. Furthermore, the values underpinning the change, the perspective adopted by existing policy (written or unwritten), and the initiators of change are crucial to its final success.

Having discussed the change process, the next stage is making decisions about how it can be put into effect. Against a background of philosophical values, the practical term 'planning' must intervene. Agreements arrived at through consensus, put into an achievable time scale, are fundamental if the change is to have any effect on the school.

All this talk of theory, philosophy, values and planning will not mean very much in developmental terms unless a simple model is adopted around which the long term developments can take place and flourish. Such a model can be seen in Figure 5.1, 'A Framework for Development'. In the framework a number of discussion phases are interspersed with appropriate action phases, as can be seen from the diagram. Progress between these two major phases is achieved by the application of a series of tactics. Each tactic is an activity specifically designed to bring about a course of action so that progress can be made through the framework. For example it could be a workshop, a visit, the evaluation of material and so on. For simplicity, those which facilitate discussion have been referred to as discussion tactics and those which bring about a course of action, as action tactics.

An important feature of the framework is its flexible application in the management of the change process. It is designed to be applied in a variety of situations, each requiring the use of different sets of tactics which provide the flexibility already referred to. Additionally, entry into the framework can be at any point according to the needs of those involved. Gradually as confidence grows in the users of the framework, its flexibility will be appreciated. In some instances, it may be appropriate to foreshorten or miss out some of the stages and lengthen others.

The timescale and pace of progress through the framework are clearly the responsibility of the headteacher as only he/she will know when to proceed to the next phase. Similarly, the roles which various people play in relation to each phase are important. The question of timescale in relation to the successful use of the framework for the benefit of *all* pupils presupposes that *all* teachers in a school are involved in the

Figure 5.1: A Framework for Development

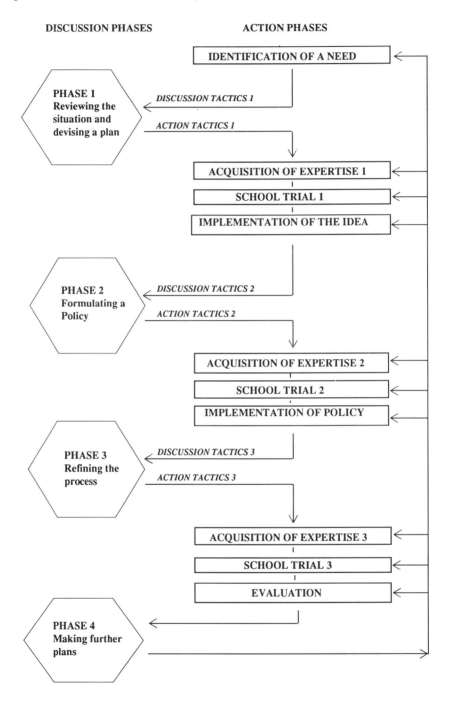

development. It has been found that the framework can be applied equally well to major or minor change processes.

An example of a minor change process could be something which an individual teacher is trying to sort out in their own classroom situation. In a minor way the curriculum development framework can be applied to sort out the problem and may, in some instances, lead to discussion amongst the staff. For example, the staff as a group in the discussion phase may have already been considering issues related to the organization of their classrooms. An individual teacher as a result of this discussion may plan to use the tactic of re-positioning her desk and subsequently, in the school trial, monitor the effort that this has on classroom organization.

An example of a fairly major application of the framework might be if a school has identified the need to centralize resources for science and design technology. From discussions held in the school between the staff it can be seen that the science and design technology curriculum might be supported better if all children could have access to a wider range of resources. Almost certainly in a case of this kind some staff will agree with the identified need and enthusiastically back it whilst other staff may not be so supportive.

In order to get the model working effectively, a whole series of tactics need to be used. After some discussion informally in the staff room (Discussion Tactic 1), it may be decided that some of the enthusiasts should prepare a paper for the staff so that they can review the situation and thereby enter phase one of the discussion. Provided that general agreement is reached during this discussion phase, resulting in the devising of a plan, the next tactic used may well be to ask the same member of staff, or even a group of the staff, to carry out the research necessary to find out how best the resources can be centralized (Action Tactic 1). If more than one member of staff is involved, they may have to seek information from books, visit other schools and centres which have been involved in centralizing their resource provision and perhaps seek the help of a consultant external to the school (Acquisition of Expertise 1).

When all this has been achieved and the ideas tried (School Trial 1), then the staff concerned will need to discuss their findings with others. If agreement is reached at this stage, then this group or another group can be detailed to make a start on the centralization of resource items. The action phase which refers to the Implementation of the Idea could well involve the action tactic of all teachers agreeing to meet on a particular day in school and removing from the shelves and cupboards in their classrooms all the items which they feel could be stored centrally.

At the same time, it may be appropriate for the school policy to be modified, or the notion of centralized resource use written into a policy statement. Once this stage has been reached, then the tactic which might be used to refine the process could be the organization of the resource items by cataloguing and colour coding the items concerned (School Trial 2). After a period of time has elapsed and the system is used (Implementation of Policy), the staff will need to meet together to evaluate how effective the new resource arrangement is working and enter the discussion phase about refining the process.

With the advent of Local Management of Schools (LMS) it might even be possible for a larger primary school to organize its financial resources in such a way that a little extra help can be provided to run the resource provision. Phase four of the curriculum development framework might also make a provision for the idea that more resources contained in classrooms should be centralized in a similar way to those used to support the science and design technology curriculum. Tactics attached to the action phases might also include the use of an external change agent to discuss and identify ways of improving the curriculum provision or, alternatively, another tactic may well be the school reacting to a comment made by an Advisor/Inspector who has visited the school.

The advantage of this particular developmental framework is that it can be applied to almost any situation where there is a need for change. It might have been used to work out the requirements for assessing pupil performance at the key age stages in the core subjects required by the National Curriculum. Evaluation in this case would be on a much wider scale involving parents, politicians, governors and professionals. The reader is left to apply his/her imagination to fill in what the rest of the stages could be. It remains to be seen what the outcomes of this particular aspect of the National Curriculum might be.

The use of a variety of tactics in applying the framework as illustrated above provides a mechanism for teachers to learn how to change. For example, one tactic which has been widely used by external change agents, working with schools in an INSET capacity, has been to devise a workshop from which the staff may acquire knowledge or develop a particular view. One particular workshop which has been used frequently is reproduced in Discussion Tactics 1, page 134 and attempts to engage the staff of the school in the important discussion of, 'What Do We Mean by Science and Design Technology Education?' Experience has shown that frequently teachers in the primary sector do not have a common notion of science and design technology education as it is applied to the needs of younger pupils. The style of the workshop promotes free discussion amongst those involved to establish a common understanding of education which perhaps would not have taken place in any other way.

The process of change outlined above involving discussion and action on the part of the staff of the school is a good example of a staff having the tenacity and ability to learn how to change. This is perhaps as important as the change itself. It is out of such detailed discussion that the need for careful planning will emerge. To begin with, it is desirable that the staff subscribe to a corporate plan in order to identify their ownership of any action which follows. Within this overall structure there will be a need for individuals to work their own way forward. A process of planning is fundamental to effective change.

The Need for Effective Leadership

The model described above is a curriculum development framework which is non-threatening since it allows considerable scope for local decision making and flexibility of use. It is also a management model for change since leadership is crucial to its implementation. Leadership here implies the headteacher, though this need not always be the case; it could well be a member of staff who has taken on the role of curriculum leader or even someone outside the school. For the duration of the change process through to implementation of that particular change, discussion will be necessary to assess the effect the change will have on the statement of policy.

No school, however small it may be, can enter into a change process without effective leadership. Of course the role of the leader will change according to the size of the school. The headteacher of a very small village school may only be the leader of one or two other staff whilst maintaining a teaching commitment for himself/herself. In the case of a larger primary school, the head will almost certainly be in a non-teaching role for most of the time. Many heads, however, even in the larger schools, will ensure that they have regular contact with all of the pupils. Developments associated with the implementation of curriculum change will only take place in schools where the question of leadership has been sorted out. It is inappropriate to analyze here the styles of leadership which can be attributed to different types of headteacher. It is, however, important to establish that significant development of the curriculum, leading to school improvement, is about exercising a collaborative form of leadership. Clearly the headteacher, who is at the centre of a school's value system, will exercise a particular style of leadership which will have a significant influence on the way in which the school develops. The influence which parents and the community exert in the context and culture of the school is also important and it should be noted and recognized. The aspect of the headteacher's role which needs to be looked at in more detail in the context of development is that of 'leading professional'.

First of all, a headteacher contemplating development and change must make a judgment about whether the time is right even to enter a commitment; there are often very good reasons why such a judgment should be made against proceeding further. Second, a decision has to be made about entering into a developmental commitment which may last a long time. It is no good contemplating a developmental sequence of this magnitude and complexity if it is not to be seen through to an ultimate conclusion: a changing policy backed by the permanent implementation of change. Too many primary schools have, in the past, entered the 'grand tour' of the curriculum and embarked on another subject before they have really finished the development of the first idea.

Developmental commitments of this kind need to be decided upon collaboratively by the head in discussion with the whole staff, or a single member. In some instances the head or a member of staff may wish to have this collaborative exercise conducted with an external consultant involved. At this very early stage it is important that provisional goal-setting should focus very clearly on the improvement of curricular experiences for the pupils. With goals established, sensitive handling of the discussion about the change, even with a stranger in the group, will often persuade a staff group to become involved. The identification of roles, time scales, workloads and a sensitive appreciation of colleagues' strengths and weaknesses is important and should be awarded discussion time by the whole group.

All of this important preliminary preparation needs to be handled carefully and documented. It is very easy to dispute agreements which have been made at an early stage if they remain verbal and are not recorded. In addition to seeing that records are kept and distributed to all the staff, the head must take on another crucially important role, that of 'pace maker'. The pace of development entered into conscientiously by a primary school is an interesting study. No worthy developmental situation should ignore the life and culture of the school. We all know that, at certain times of the year, whole school activities tend to slow down developments of this kind. It may be necessary for the staff of the school, which has been following the curriculum framework as a guide, to agree to suspend major developments at the 'acquisition of expertise' stage and wait until a colleague has taken secondment to attend a course which will provide the necessary skills and knowledge for the development to proceed. Similarly, time will be necessary to prepare and produce a Christmas concert or school play.

In most primary schools, certainly the smaller schools, the headteacher's leadership will exert an influence in the school setting by concentrating on the *process* of leading. Leading by example, should occupy a dominant place within the head's management behaviour towards the achievement of change. The head's personality, his/her particular values and competences continue to be seen as major factors in determining the quality of the school. Personal qualities which appreciate contributions made by colleagues, either by accepting them or by dealing with them in a constructively critical way, can ensure that development is supported by the full involvement of everyone concerned.

It should be seen that the model described is collaborative which, in developmental terms, provides the most fruitful outcome for all the pupils. However, an imposed change can work in the same way although it does not immediately engender the same kind of willingness and mutual support within the staff group. Such imposition from outside the school may meet with opposition, policy requirements imposed by the LEA or Central Government may fall into this category. The National Curriculum could fall into this category also, but it is predicted that when teachers learn that it is generally supportive of good practice and provides a framework for implementation over a period of time, they will struggle hard to meet the requirements laid down.

The National Curriculum will mean that those schools with an existing curriculum policy for science and design technology will need to carry out a review process, and those schools who have yet to develop policy in these areas will find that it gives useful guidelines. Good schools will also see the need to develop and adapt any policy to their own needs, reflecting the needs, content and culture of the school. Incorporated into their institutional policy will be the recognition of any policy requirements of the LEA as well as the National Curriculum. The developmental leadership in the school will need to plan and act within the context of the policy for change which outlines the general aims of the school and also develop specific detailed policy relating to the science and design technology curriculum. Planning for this kind of policy change will need to be sequential, systematic and take place over an extended time scale. Someone in the school must take on the responsibility for planning and replanning so that continuity of improvement is maintained. Records are essential in this process, as a key member of staff may leave with the consequent loss of continuity of development and experiences which the children have gained. Every effort should be made to ensure this kind of 'hiccup' does not happen, or its effect minimized when it does occur.

Much has already been said about the role of the headteacher in terms of his/her leadership of such developments (Holly & Southworth, 1989). It is also within the power of the headteacher to delegate responsibility to a member of staff for a particular reason. Such delegation should not only involve the task itself but also the delegation of the responsibility to see the task through to some logical and productive outcome. Teachers are more likely to grow professionally when they are given complete responsibility by a headteacher. They have to learn how to adapt to the requirements of delegated responsibility and find out by experience how to negotiate issues with the staff as a whole or with individuals. The role of curriculum leader, under the new structure for payment of allowances to teachers, is an interesting one. The delegated responsibility from the head may be to a deputy in a small school or a teacher on main professional grade in a larger school. Whatever the size of school involved, the developmental role is quite a difficult one to play; it is perhaps more difficult to exercise the role in a smaller school than a large school where the relationships between teachers, head, pupils and parents tend to be very close. Whoever is playing the role of curriculum leader will very quickly learn that ideas and knowledge need to be shared if progress is to be made towards cooperative thinking within the school. If the curriculum leader does not learn quickly that in exercising responsibility, tact and diplomacy are two useful qualities to develop, his/her method of operating will perhaps appear threatening to the staff with consequent undesirable effects on their willingness to cooperate. Real responsibility delegated to another person by the headteacher will involve that individual not only in cooperating with the head, but also with members of staff, with individual children whom he/she may be teaching and with staff based centrally within the Authority such as advisers and advisory teachers.

Any matters requiring decisions, particularly those which may affect the policy of the school, will need to be discussed with the headteacher first and then maybe with the staff at a later stage. From this discussion of the role of the curriculum leader, it is perhaps becoming apparent that change can be implemented by agreement at a particular time or it can take place progressively, which should allow all the members of staff to develop professionally and adopt a collaborative, creative approach to the teaching and learning situation.

The implementation of change shown in Figure 5.2 shows the key role which the staff play in the implementation of change. It also recognizes that time should be found for productive professional discussion to be held at a time when the teachers are free from the responsibility of taking a class of children.

About ten years ago, it was felt that one area of Bedfordshire was ready for the curriculum framework to be tried out. The change agents were approached by a group of primary school headteachers and a sessional in-service course was arranged for the fourteen schools involved. Each session was held in a different school so that those invited, the head plus one other teacher, could learn something new from the visit. When the course was completed, the heads decided to set up a working party to advise the whole group on the best way to continue development through to the stage of permanent implementation of change.

After about six months, the convener of the group of heads contacted one of the course leaders and indicated that not only had no progress been made, but the working party felt that they had exhausted all possibilities and really needed some guidance. A meeting was set up to discuss the impasse. Quickly it was established that the working party had moved along the cul-de-sac of trying to produce a common 'syllabus' for science activities and found that it was an impossible task. Their intention of producing a syllabus was that once they had achieved a simple statement of content, they could share it with the other schools in the area and their task would be complete. After one or two more meetings the working party was becoming convinced of the need to produce something a little different to share with their fellow heads in the area. These discussions gave rise to the need to produce something which would help others realize that the process was more complex and it was really to do with the implementation of change. Such a process is summarized in Figure 5.2.

It should be noted that the following points are also key to the development:

1   The 'driving force' is the energy and willingness amongst a group to want to change something. It could very well be the way in which the science curriculum is approached, but could also easily be a completely different area of the curriculum being considered.

2   The central role of the headteacher must be recognized in any development of this kind. The policy, at school and local level, is arrived at by a process of consultation and discussion.

3   After a joint decision has been reached about the implementation of an aspect of policy under discussion, the head then becomes a member of the 'staff'. In

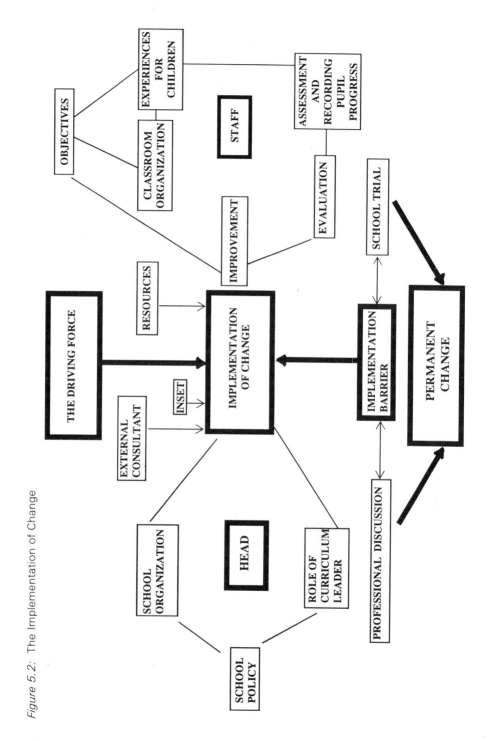

Figure 5.2: The Implementation of Change

instances where the head has withdrawn from the school trial stage, the full implementation of policy tends to be aborted. The head, of course, may choose to take on another role, that of evaluator, which will necessitate much observation of the trial stage and subsequent reporting back to the whole staff group.

4   On more than one occasion it has been found that a strange phenomenon occurs if the staff have been busily discussing changes formally in the staff room. The conversation becomes so intense in some instances that a phobia develops about trying things out; it is as if a 'barrier' is erected which must be removed in some way before even the temporary implementation of an idea is tried out in the classroom.

5   After, however, the barrier has been crossed forwards and backwards on several occasions, between professional discussion and temporary implementation then, and perhaps only then, is permanent change likely to have taken place. Once a permanent change has taken place it should be reflected in the school policy.

Figure 5.2 shows clearly that progress in implementing change is only made when the driving force exceeds the force represented by the implementation barrier.

The reward for becoming involved with this kind of developmental process is that the school becomes a lively and dynamic place in which the work of professionals and pupils becomes exciting and rewarding. By constantly evaluating and re-evaluating aspects of policy which have been implemented through a change process, the optimism of the school will also be maintained. A creative and dynamic approach to the place of learning is difficult to maintain but when it is attributable to the skills which the professional staff as a whole exert on one another within a primary school, it is easily recognized by the happiness which is shown on the faces of the pupils.

An advantage to be gained by those professionals involved in a developmental situation is that not only do they grow professionally but also they grow sufficiently to contemplate career development by taking on more senior roles themselves. Although much can be learned in the place of work about the complexities of the whole school approach to development, it is necessary for those contemplating a leadership role within a school to embark upon a course which will help them develop their skills and thinking. Courses developed for headteachers, deputies and curriculum coordinators to look at their management style imply that it is possible to train teachers for such tasks. Training can convey the idea that all individuals have to do to develop into such a demanding role is to acquire information about its demands. This is very wide of the mark, as the best courses concentrate on the development of the individual as well as giving and sharing information about systems of management. Such preparation for leadership is essential if change is to be effected. Furthermore it should be seen as part of the ongoing LEA provision which schools can utilize as part of a rolling programme of development outlined in their National Curriculum Development Plans.

The Role of the LEA

For those who already occupy leadership posts in primary schools, another form of support is growing quickly within LEAs. The advisory function of LEA Inspection/Advisory services is being carried out more adequately with support from advisory teachers. One inspector can therefore exert an influence in developmental terms by managing a small team of advisory teachers who, in time, take on the whole responsibility for developmental work as an external consultant to schools. Such collaboration between schools and the LEA will be an important feature in the establishment of the National Curriculum. Governing bodies working with the headteacher of a school will be responsible for asking questions about the application to and development of various areas of the curriculum. Not only will the head need the support of his/her district inspector but will also expect support from teachers acting in an advisory capacity who can work alongside themselves or members of staff in the classroom.

The role of the advisory teacher, as outlined, is crucial to ensure the development of a relevant science and design technology curriculum to all pupils within an Authority's primary schools. It is predicted that such support will need to continue in this area of the curriculum for sometime to come and it is imperative that an LEA understands it own role in the development of the curriculum.

> Only in curricular form can ideas be tested by teachers. Curricula are hypothetical procedures testable only in classrooms. (Lawrence Stenhouse)

> Only teachers can create good teaching, and thus it is imperative that they occupy a central role in developing curriculum and that they develop with a curriculum. (David Hopkins)

These two quotes have been included to proceed a look at Figure 5.3, 'The Development of Curriculum Policy'. Expressed in diagrammatic form, the curricular policy of a school tends to look overshadowed by the provisions made by Central and Local Government, and by the INSET provision made by various people and agencies. However, there are several innovations which are depicted on the diagram:

1   The school is now required to express its curriculum in policy terms. This is a different method of expressing a curriculum to that which has hitherto been required.
2   The curriculum development process which supports and develops the curriculum of the school is now very definitely school-focused. Courses which are now provided by various agencies have to be designed with the needs of the classroom and the pupils very much in mind. Often, more advanced degrees and diplomas will demand that the student carries out research in the classroom situation.
3   Both the curriculum policy of the school and the LEA must receive approval of either the governors or the members of the LEA.
4   The role of inspectors/advisors will move more towards monitoring and evaluation of the policies of both the LEA and the school in curricular terms. Working with HMI, they will also be required to monitor the effects of the National Curriculum.
5   The INSET provision made available through various agencies will continue to be supported in the future by specifically targeted Education Support Grant finance made available directly from Central Government sources to the LEA.

With such pressure and support outside the school, the educational needs of individual children, many of whom will begin to live their adult lives in the next century, should be

Figure 5.3: The Development of Curriculum Policy

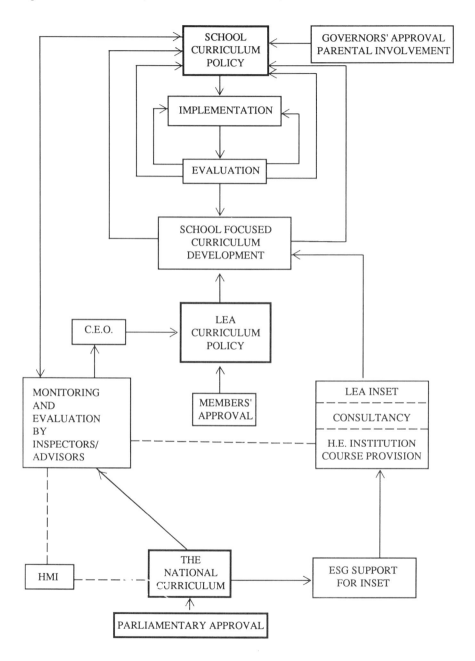

should be adequately addressed. The evaluative process applied to the development of curriculum policy nationally, locally and at school level will ensure that curriculum development will not only be progressive and continuous but should also reflect the needs of a society which is becoming increasingly scientific and technologically minded.

The Need for INSET

Shortly after a group of staff have become involved with changes to their practice, with subsequent evaluation of the application, they realize that the change process needs to be accompanied by relevant in-service course provision. At this point in the discussion, if the staff see the need for the Curriculum Development Framework to be used as the driving force for the implementation of change, see Figure 5.4, *a very powerful tool has been acquired by the group*.

If the staff of a school have worked their way through these four phases using the implementation of change idea, driven by the curriculum development framework, then they should, as a school, have progressed considerably in terms of permanent implementation of change. Changes in the policy, applied to the science and design technology curriculum, will be a consequence of this.

Any INSET provision which is designed to bring about such enormous change needs to be based upon a particular rationale. A rationale for INSET is necessary because any changes in curriculum terms require that individuals learn to do something new. The rationale adopted by Bedfordshire in the application of the Curriculum Development Framework is as follows:

INSET should:
— work towards the implementation of science and design technology in all classes within a school.
— help teachers provide activities for children which will help them develop certain personal qualities, basic concepts and skills and acquire knowledge.
— help teachers provide for progression of individuals within a class and within a school.
— help teachers evaluate their own teaching.

The following experiences have been important in shaping the current INSET provision:

The modification of the INSET provision towards that which is school-focused and often school-based led to the understanding that the implementation of change requires ongoing professional development activity within the school, backed up by advanced level provision supported by the LEA.

By providing workshop courses for headteachers and teachers and ensuring that within these courses other headteachers and teachers were reporting on their developmental experiences, progress was made. The notion that teachers will learn and understand best by being coached by other teachers is true; this leaves the role of the external providers of INSET mainly that of training the trainers.

When developmental strategies are applied to an LEA and its schools in a systematic way it is quickly realized that the quality of INSET is more important than the quantity.

Figure 5.4: The Driving Force for Change

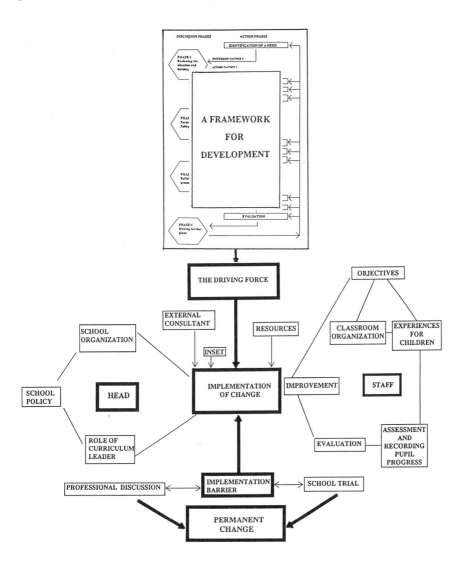

The requirement to implement a policy at the different levels does have the effect of making the professional role more dynamic but at the same time more demanding; as a consequence it makes the school a more interesting place in which to work and therefore provides the necessary challenges to interesting and lively children.

In drawing this chapter to a close, the reader should begin to acquire a view of how school-focused INSET can work within the school and within the Authority. To support this view the following remarks were made by Michael Fullan (1986):

. . . a new task focused, continuous professional development, combining a variety of learning formats, and a variety of trainers and other support personnel is evolving and is effective in bringing about change in practice.

. . . there is some evidence to show that a small amount of time, used under the right conditions over a period of several months, alternating between practice and training, can go a long way.

Chapter 6

Managing Change Within a School in the Long Term

Introduction

In formulating an overall policy for development, once a school or school group has identified the required change (in this case the implementation of the National Curriculum in science and design technology), accepted that the capacity for change lies within itself and that it needs to be 'pro-active' in the use of outside assistance, it is then in a position to consider the next stage in the process.

In the short term, some change has already taken place in all schools, since Key Stage 1 of the National Curriculum was implemented in September 1989. In the long term, however, if permanent change is to occur, a strategy for implementation of the development policy has to be identified within the planning framework and time scale for implementation which best meets the needs of the school as a whole. Over a number of years, the framework described earlier in chapter 5, has been shown to be an effective planning vehicle in a variety of situations. Schools will not regret applying this, at least, as a starting point for development particularly since it has been conceived as a result of a sound understanding of the change process and is based upon the premise that review needs to proceed development. Its use also incorporates other important requirements in implementing change, those of ongoing professional development activity within the school, the acceptance of adequate resourcing, the need for effective leadership and the use of a built-in evaluative mechanism.

Readers will remember that in working towards the identified need, that of formulating and implementing a policy for the development of a particular curricular area, in this case science and design technology, schools move via a series of discussion and action phases. Time scale and rate of progress through the framework are clearly the responsibility of the headteacher. Also, according to the stage of development of the school, it may be appropriate to foreshorten some of the stages and lengthen others. A crucial factor in the success of the development lies in the interspersing of the 'action' phases, described above, with the 'discussion' phases. It is during these that progress can be accelerated and flexibility, relating to the needs of a specific school, can be provided by the existence of a wide range of tactics, mainly in the form of school-based workshops. (Guidelines for these are included in Part 2.) Using a manipulative strategy, appropriate programmes of 'discussion' and 'action' phases are negotiated, enabling staff to undertake the development of the curriculum in a way which is most meaningful to them and, thus, most likely to be implemented.

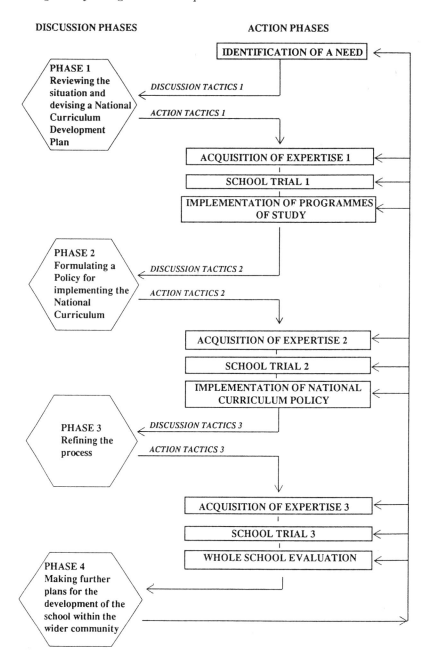

Figure 6.1: A Framework for Development of the National Curriculum in Primary Science and Design Technology

Clearly, the framework provides an invaluable mechanism for formulating, implementing and evaluating a school's National Curriculum Development Plan.

Figure 6.1 provides a version of the framework described earlier which has been adapted specifically to help schools bring about the changes necessary to implement the National Curriculum in primary science and design technology. The fine details of each phase are outlined below.

Framework for Development of the National Curriculum in Primary Science and Design Technology

Discussion Phase 1: Reviewing the Situation in the School and Devising a National Curriculum Development Plan

Whatever the stage of development of the school, discussion phase 1 must always be used as a starting point. This phase has been designed to give the opportunity to address a number of the crucial issues outlined below and, as a result, devise a National Curriculum Development Plan.

Discussion Phase 1: Reviewing the Situation

Acccountability
    Why science and design technology are included in the National Curriculum.

Planning
    Identifying needs — *What* needs to be done?

    Who needs to know more about:

    Science and design technology process?
    Appropriate key concepts, attitudes, skills and knowledge?
    Appropriate activities with children?
    Organization of science and technology activities?
    Appropriate resources?

    Responding to needs — *How* can we do it?
    Formulating the programme — *When* will it be appropriate?

Coordination
    Who will lead the development?
    What will his/her role be?
    Can this person start immediately?
    Does he/she need further training?

    Is there a need for outside support?
    Will an advisory teacher be needed to start things off?
    Will consultancy support suffice?
    Will we need to ask for additional resources?

Initially, in considering *accountability*, although science and design technology have now been included in the basic curriculum, it is necessary for all staff to come to terms with the underlying philosophy for their inclusion. Only then will they be able to teach to some purpose and be truly accountable to parents, governors and others. The workshop in Part 2 (Discussion Tactics 1) is designed to help with this issue.

Next, as part of the *Planning* exercise, it is important to ascertain the nature and level of the additional expertise required by staff. One way of finding out is to ask colleagues informally. A perceptive headteacher and knowledgeable science coordinator will also know who needs to take advantage of professional development opportunities. Another way is to administer a questionnaire similar to the one reproduced in Part 2 (Discussion Tactics 1). If the staff of the school are prepared to be honest, then such a document, administered anonymously, can be a source of valuable information. Alternatively, teachers can fill it in according to perceived expectations! In either case teachers involved in trying out the questionnaire were assured that, at least, it served to raise the relevant issues and, at most, provide insight as to the way forward. For some it acted as a self-evaluative tool.

Having established felt needs and given some thought to the kind of response which might be made in Action Phase 1, it is now necessary to determine which can be met through collaborative school-focused and school-based INSET and which require the rigour of a more substantial, centrally-based course. With regard to the latter, outside support, from the relevant inspector/adviser is of value since he/she should be in a position not only to support individual teachers but also to advise them on the centrally-based course which best meets their requirements and the needs of the school. Often, where a large investment of money is at stake, teachers may well be asked if they are prepared to pass on the expertise gained to colleagues in schools other than their own. A period of negotiation may thus take place in planning a way forward, since such a requirement not only affects the teacher concerned but also may well put pressure on his/her school due to the possibility of an increased work load.

For those needs which can be met internally, it is all the more important to determine a plan of action for a school-based INSET programme (Action Phase 'Acquisition of Expertise'), built into which is the implementation of the ideas explored within the school (Action Phase: 'School Trial'). This will represent the first stage in the implementation of a school's National Curriculum Development Plan. Requirements will need to be prioritized and the programme paced in order to allow individual expertise to be gained, to spread the pressure put upon individual teachers and to allow for consolidation to take place in between sessions. Of prime importance here is the realization that to develop too much at any one time can be counter-productive. Teachers should only be asked to take small steps in the change process and headteachers should give them every opportunity to concentrate their efforts. For example, it might be better to concentrate on only one of the National Currriculum key stages at first. A consideration of developing the core curriculum as part of topic work is another possibility. In a school with a large number of teachers requiring individual support, such a programme might extend over two or three terms. Therefore, it must clearly take its place along with other curricular areas, as part of a long term professional development programme designed to meet the priorities of the National Curriculum and the school as a whole in its quest to seek further improvement.

Schools at an early stage of development will need to embark on a programme of first level training (Action Phase: 'Acquisition of Expertise 1'). This is concerned largely with the involvement of staff in a number of after school workshops which raise awareness and help with the implementation of new teaching/learning styles, in individual classrooms. Schools will need to have very clear objectives if they are to identify those workshops which will help them the most and they will then have to build them into the programme, allowing time for those requiring the corporate classroom feedback which is so valuable in the staff team building process. A selection of workshops is included in Part 2 (Action Tactics 1) and schools would be well advised to consider the issues raised here as a starting point. It is accepted, however, that some schools will be ready to enter into Discussion Phase 2 and embark on second level training (Action Phase: 'Acquisition of Expertise 2') involving the higher order skills of assessment, matching and record keeping described in Part 2 (Action Tactics 2).

Alongside and parallel to this, schools may also like to consider supplementing this programme with a series of visits to other schools or resource centres. Such activity can be funded through the GRIST Consortium arrangements, provided it is part of a predetermined plan, and can provide the basis for a stimulating 'report back' session. Teachers will find that a small amount of this activity will go a long way to helping them clarify their needs.

In a consideration of the issue of *coordination*, the major implications are that INSET, of necessity, has a long time scale, should be school-based, relates directly to the needs of the school concerned and involves the whole school staff. This includes the headteacher, whose role is crucial to its success, and another teacher, the coordinator, who is expected, at some point in time, to lead the development. It is accepted, however, that in small schools this role may well be taken on by the headteachers.

At this stage, it is crucial that not only is the person identified but that also their role is carefully defined, not only as perceived by him/herself, but also by the headteacher and by the colleagues with whom he/she will be expected to work. A workshop which will help all concerned to identify the major facets involved, is included in Part 2 (Discussion Tactics 1). It will also serve the purpose of deciding whether the coordinator has sufficient expertise to lead right away or whether further training is required. The training which coordinators undergo enables them to identify the needs of their own colleagues, familiarizes them with the responses required and provides them with the management skills necessary to take on a leadership role.

A decision on the above also relates to the question of the need for and nature of outside support, particularly in terms of initially leading the development. Currently in Bedfordshire, several approaches are taken which are distinguished only by the point in time when the coordinator actually takes over the process of change.

In some schools, coordinators undergo a process of central training (Action Phase: 'Acquisition of Expertise 1') to ensure that they obtain sufficient knowledge of management skills to enable them to begin to take on a leadership role, within their own school, from the beginning. In such cases, additional consultative support can be provided from outside the school when required. Similarly the LEA should take on a monitoring role. Such is the situation, represented in Figure 6.2, which all schools should begin to work towards.

In other schools, the establishment of an internal coordinator is more gradual and the major curriculum development input is imposed from outside initially, with a coordinator undergoing training alongside colleagues as shown in Figure 6.3. In time, the school

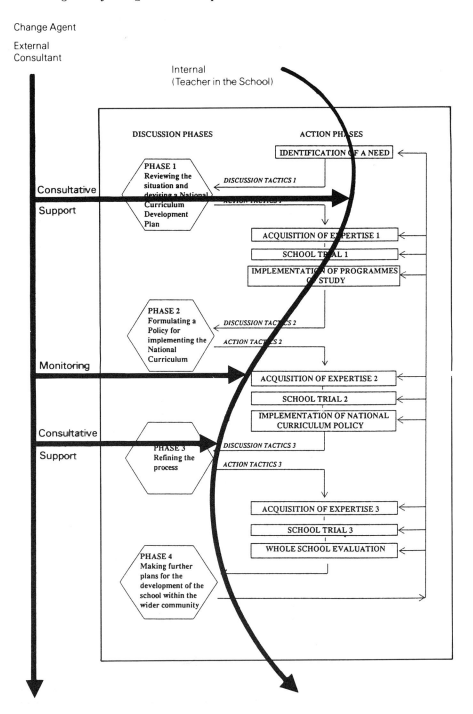

Figure 6.2: The Use of Occasional External Support

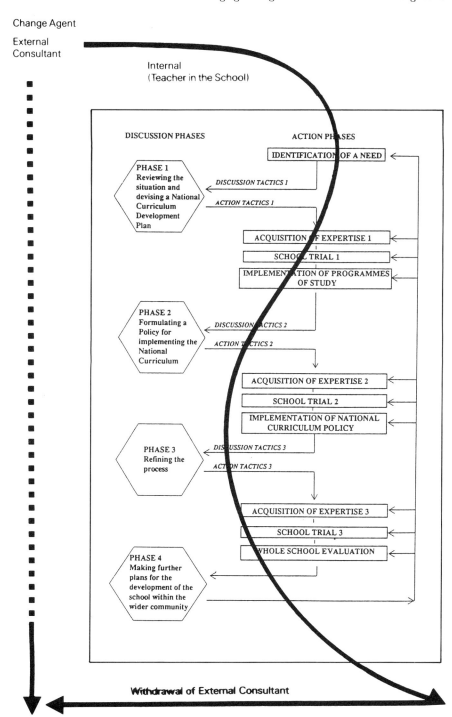

Figure 6.3: The Use of Total External Support

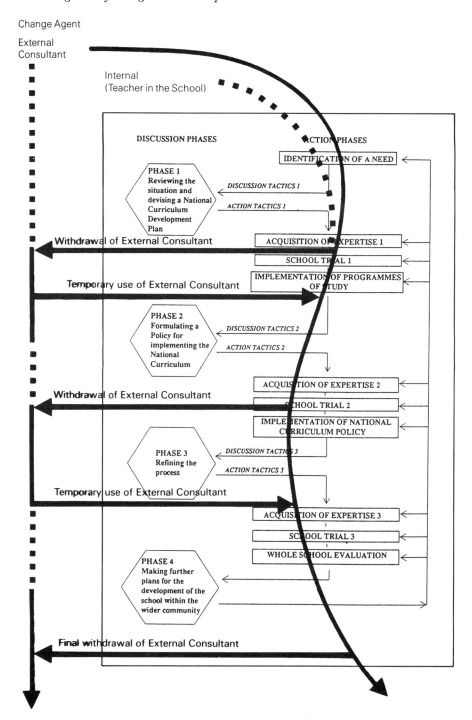

Figure 6.4: The Use of Partial External Support

coordinator takes over, knowing that outside support can be provided when necessary, as indicated in Figure 6.4. Eventually the transfer of immediate responsibility for the development is complete, including the ongoing dissemination of skills acquired to the whole staff.

Initially, it is usual for each school to rely heavily on an external support system whose quality is crucial to the success of the change process. This includes accessibility to appropriate 'process' and management oriented, centrally-based courses which enable individuals to increase their own expertise, and the immediate availability of a wide range of resources which must be varied in the subject matter and suitable for a wide ability range of both teachers and children. Most importantly, an effective consultancy service must operate with access to advisory teacher support at staffroom and classroom levels. At a later point in time, a wider experience and growing confidence enables most teachers to become self supporting and an 'after care' programme is all that may be required.

Action Phase 1

Having involved colleagues in discussion at all levels, schools will now be in a position to move into the first implementation phase of the programme. Plans for individual teachers to acquire expertise can be put into operation and the desired school-based, first-level training programme can commence (Acquisition of Expertise 1).

As indicated earlier, in Bedfordshire primary and middle schools, school-based INSET programmes concerned with first level training have been administered either internally, by the school's own coordinator, or externally by advisory teachers. In the latter case, as well as having a consultancy role, the advisory teacher is responsible for teaching a number of after-school course sessions, designed to meet the felt needs of the school, which are also supported by team teaching aimed at the professional development of individual staff. The value of such a method of working is that issues discussed on the course can then be firmly related to classroom practice, making it more likely that changes made will be sustained. Where school coordinators take on this role, they may need to undergo management training on a centrally based course prior to leading the initiative. Support in the form of team teaching is then provided by a member of the advisory teacher team or the school coordinator, using GRIST Consortium funding.

Experience to date has shown that adequate first level training can be accomplished in about six after-school sessions of one to one and a half hours duration. If this can be supplemented with team teaching in the classroom, as described earlier, the rate of progress will undoubtedly be accelerated. A consideration of what is meant by science and design technology education (see Part 2, Action Tactics 1) provides an excellent focus for the first session and, for schools at an early stage of development, it has been found valuable to agree upon a whole school topic on which to base the work. This can be implemented (school trial 1) for a period which best suits the age range of the children and has the advantage that teachers not only acquire a common vocabulary, but can also begin to look at progression within the school. In this context, the programmes of study and attainment targets identified in the National Curriculum document, can be invaluable.

The selection of further workshops (see Part 2 Action Tactics 1) will depend upon the particular needs of the school, but it must be stressed that progress will only be made if each session has clear objectives. Meeting together and discussing issues informally without a

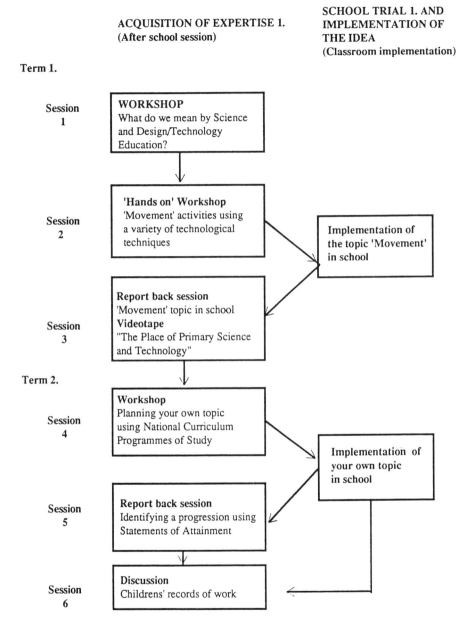

Figure 6.5: Action Phase 1: A School-based Programme for Science and Design Technology

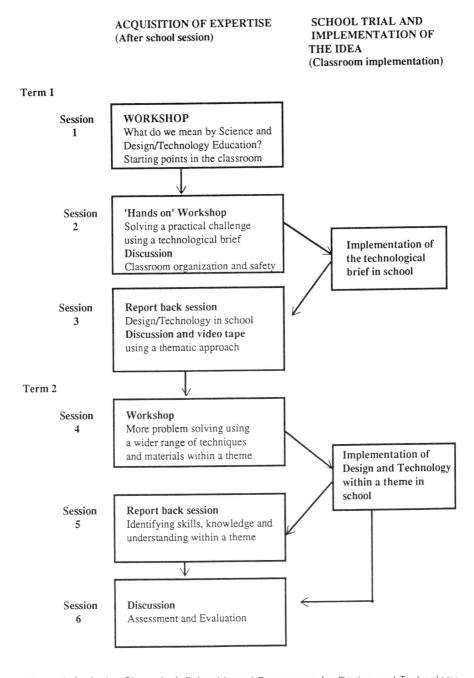

ACQUISITION OF EXPERTISE
(After school session)

**SCHOOL TRIAL AND
IMPLEMENTATION OF
THE IDEA**
(Classroom implementation)

Term 1

Session
1

WORKSHOP
What do we mean by Science and
Design/Technology Education?
Starting points in the classroom

Session
2

'Hands on' Workshop
Solving a practical challenge
using a technological brief
Discussion
Classroom organization and safety

**Implementation of
the technological
brief in school**

Session
3

Report back session
Design/Technology in school
Discussion and video tape
using a thematic approach

Term 2

Session
4

Workshop
More problem solving using
a wider range of techniques
and materials within a theme

**Implementation of
Design and Technology
within a theme in
school**

Session
5

Report back session
Identifying skills, knowledge and
understanding within a theme

Session
6

Discussion
Assessment and Evaluation

Figure 6.6: Action Phase 1: A School-based Programme for Design and Technology

each session has clear objectives. Meeting together and discussing issues informally without a pre-imposed structure will only lead to frustration and the eventual breakdown of the development. Figure 6.5 represents a typical, level one training programme.

The workshops in term one are designed not only to consider the philosophy of Primary Science and Design Technology education but also to 'break the ice'. If, during this term, the whole school topic can be resourced from outside the school or by the coordinator, then teachers can concentrate on the science and design technology teaching rather than on the much lower level but laborious activity of collecting the necessary bits and pieces together to enable children to carry out the activities. This also has the effect of raising the level of motivation of individuals and does not expose them too much in terms of meeting resource demands.

During the second term, having gained in confidence, they can then begin gradually to take over the whole responsibility for the provision of appropriate learning experiences based upon the programmes of study identified in the National Curriculum. The person leading the development will be on hand to act as consultant and gradually a corporate response to implementing science and design technology can be established. It is crucial, at this stage, that the school coordinator is not seen as the sole provider of ideas, equipment and materials, but rather as a friendly consultant who will provide help until individuals can become self-sufficient. Division of labour amongst a whole staff can provide a wide range of ideas and resources in a relatively short period of time, provided the coordinator is prepared to initiate and follow up the development. Also, in schools where science has been established for some time, a first level training programme might have a more technological bias as illustrated in Figure 6.6.

Discussion Phase 2: Formulating a Policy for Implementing the National Curriculum

Only after this first level training are the participants really in a position to know which issues are relevant to formulating a school policy for the curriculum area in question and to embark on their second level training. It is accepted, however, that some schools may well be ready to start at this level, having already embarked on a curriculum development programme previously and, for them, Discussion Phase 2 will be the starting point.

The workshop outlined in Part 2 (Discussion Tactics 2) is intended to set the scene for discussion. Schools which have progressed to this level of development will be in a position to plan the way ahead through informal discussion, since fewer barriers to change will need to be overcome. Again in order to implement second level training (Acquisition of Expertise 2), a school-based INSET programme will need to be agreed.

Discussion Phase 2: Formulating a Policy for Implementing the National Curriculum

---

Assessment
  Do we need to investigate:
    Methods of assessment?
    Ways of adapting to different levels of children's thinking?

Continuity and progression
  How do we:
    Evaluate pupils' progress?
    Ensure for continuity and progression within and between schools?

Records
  Do we need to ask about:
    Keeping records?
    Kinds of pupil profile?
    How can they be used?
    How can they help us/our children?

Balance
  Do we need to decide about:
    Methods of implementing the National Curriculum?
    Incorporating balanced science within the curriculum of the school?
    Ways of helping staff implement the policy?

How can we make sure of making informed decisions?
What are the implications of our decisions?

Action Phase 2

The second level training programme (Acquisition of Expertise 2) seeks to consolidate the work and addresses the issues of whole school curriculum development, assessment, matching, continuity and progression in the context of school policy statements and the National Curriculum, pupil profiles and record keeping.

A selection of suitable workshops has been included in Part 2 (Action Tactics 2) but many schools will now be in a position to develop their own according to need. It should be noted that the period for time for implementation can be of a much shorter duration than that required for level one training, providing a consolidation period is unnecessary. A typical sequence of workshops and related classroom experiences concerned with assessment and matching is given in Figure 6.7. When sufficient time has been set aside to consider the relevant issues in the first part of this second level training and trial certain aspects (School Trial 2), a school may then be in a position to implement a school policy for science and design technology.

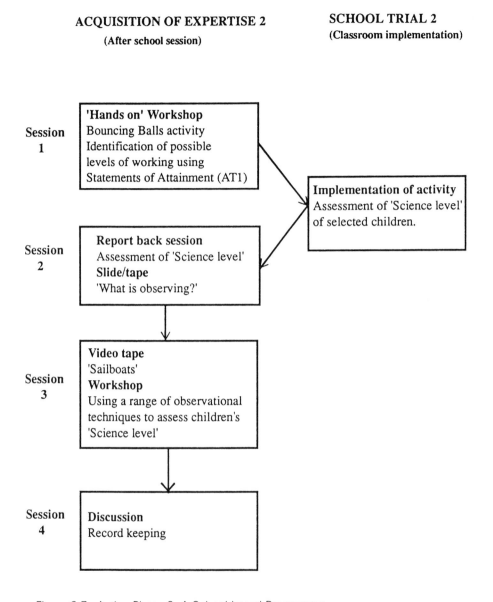

Figure 6.7: Action Phase 2: A School-based Programme

Discussion Phase 3: Refining the Process

Schools which are at a stage of development to use this phase as a starting point are already well advanced in their thinking since it is at this point that they will need to appraise the effectiveness of the policy through the process of self and school evaluation. Questions will need to be asked as follows:

Discussion Phase 3: Refining the Process

Evaluation

Is our school policy being effectively implemented?
Who needs to know ways of finding out about:

Whether their lesson was worthwhile?
What they learned?
What they should do next.?

How do we need to modify our practice?

Action Phase 3

Answers to the questions raised above in Discussion Phase 3, can best be found by following the Open University school-based INSET programme P234 'Curriculum in Action, an Approach to Evaluation' (Action Tactics 3). Slide and video-taped material is available which can be used as a focus for discussion and it is a relatively simple matter to select appropriate material from the wealth that is available in the unit. This third level training material can provide an excellent focus not only for individual teachers to appraise their own practice but also to lay the foundation for the second part of Action Phase 3, that of whole school evaluation. Figure 6.8 illustrates the variety of ways in which this process can be achieved.

As everyone knows, evaluation of the school can be externally imposed, with or without internal agreement, but by far the most important and useful form of evaluation is that which is self imposed and implemented. This type of whole school appraisal inevitably also relies on the willingness and ability of individual teachers to evaluate their own practice and undergo professional development where this is necessary.

Teachers can appraise their effectiveness through using assessment procedures and systematic record keeping to evaluate pupil performance. If it is found that a few children are failing to progress, then perhaps more care needs to be taken in matching activities to particular individuals. If, however, few of the class progress then a major review of teaching and learning styles needs to be effected.

Secondly, teachers can assess their own effectiveness in classroom management terms. It is in this respect that the Open University course is particularly valuable. Also, it is this latter form of evaluation which teachers find most rewarding since it is designed to minimize stress and maximize professional expertise.

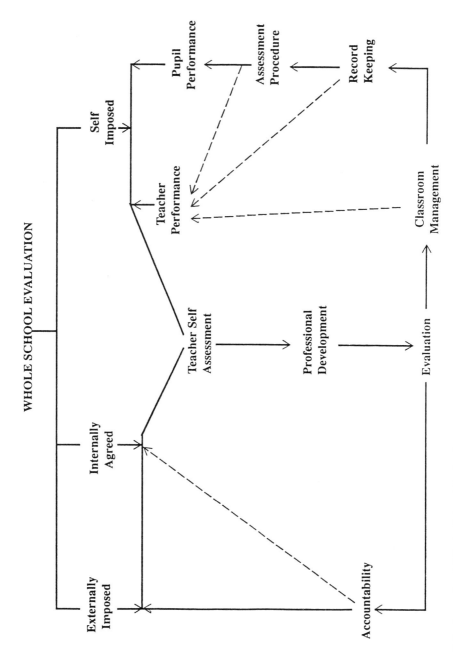

Figure 6.8: Aspects of Whole School Evaluation

Discussion Phase 4: Making Further Plans for the Development of the School Within the Wider Community

This phase, concerned as it is with further plans, is certainly the most important in terms of establishing the school as a dynamic entity within the wider community. It is relatively easy to embark upon a curriculum development programme, much more difficult to sustain it over a period of time, but it requires dedication and careful management to establish a rolling programme of curriculum review as a permanent feature of the school. Furthermore, staff must feel secure in their work with each other and immediate, free discussion of problems and innovative ideas must be allowed. This requires the building up of mutual respect and an effective system of delegation based upon known strengths of individuals. All members of staff, including the headteacher, curriculum coordinator, non-teaching assistants and other support personnel, need to feel that they are valued and that their views can be freely voiced.

All this requires a firm, but sensitive, manipulative management style which relies heavily on a knowledge of the personalities, strengths and weaknesses of individual members of the whole school team. The headteacher's role is crucial at this point.

Given that the professionalism of all concerned has developed to this extent then discussion, at this stage, should ideally focus on two facets. The way forward with regard to the evaluation of recent initiatives but also future priorities in relation to this. Questions need to be discussed as follows:

Discussion Phase 4: Making further plans

Acquisition of expertise
What future plans need to be made for the professional development of staff?

Implementation of the school policy
Are there aspects of science and design technology which have been omitted?
Does the physical organization of the school lend itself to its implementation?
Is there sufficient flexibility in teaching/learning styles?
Does the provision for matching, continuity and progression operate in practice?
Is the science and design technology and whole curriculum truly balanced?
Do the resources of the school need to be further developed?
Is the use of the school site appropriate?

Management
Do job descriptions need to be reviewed?
Does the management style need to be modified in the light of professional development of colleagues?
Is it appropriate to change methods of school-based INSET?
Is the evaluative procedure satisfactory?

Communication
Can channels of communication be improved within the school?
What provision needs to made to induct probationers and staff new to the school?
Are the liaison arrangements adequate and appropriate within and between schools?
Do strong curricular links need to be built-up with parents, governors and industry?

When the school begins to address the issues outlined above, it is obvious that others, not formally involved, will be drawn into the discussion. The school environment now needs to be widened to include the much larger local community. Only then will the work of the school take its place in the total educational continuum and be valued for the particular niche which it occupies.

Differentiation of Roles

Schools which have successfully moved through all four of these discussion and action phases will have undoubtedly grown in stature. All those involved will have developed professionally and will have changed in the process. However, an important feature in the development needs to be acknowledged, namely the recognition of the importance of the shifting nature and variety of roles which various people have assumed while applying a strategy for change. For example, a curriculum coordinator for science may be leading colleagues in INSET activities at one point. Later on, he or she becomes a participant when another area of the curriculum is being developed. If the same person attends a centrally-based course to gain expertise, he or she takes on the role of student. Differentiation of roles is a crucial feature in the application of the development framework to a particular school and must be taken into account when planning. An attempt has been made in Figure 6.9 to relate the phases of the framework to the roles of those involved with the change process.

During Discussion Phase 1, a consultation may well take place between the headteacher and an inspector/adviser during which a decision to apply the framework may be taken. Both, at this stage, take on the role of negotiator. The headteacher's role here is to establish the need for outside help and of the willingness of his/her staff to participate in a change process. Simultaneously, the head or the inspector/adviser and an advisory teacher will be researching ways in which they can meet the special needs of the school. If the initial consultation has been successful, it is essential, at an early stage, for all parties to agree a programme for the implementation of the change process.

It is now that the people involved in school should be made aware of their particular roles. The head, in determining the rate of progress of the programme, as pace controller. The staff, in maintaining momentum, as active participants. In this way a link between the school and change agents has been established. Progress can only be made if all concerned review the situation and agree to plan a strategy for change and to acquire any necessary expertise.

Since decisions made during this review phase determine the feasibility of applying the subsequent phases of the framework, it is crucial that the management of it is carefully negotiated, initially by the inspector/adviser with the head, who has now taken on the role of personnel manager. Once the basis for decision making has been established it is necessary for both to make approaches to the other groups concerned.

The advisory teacher or curriculum coordinator and school staff will need to be involved in the conscious planning of the strategy for change which should result in the temporary implementation of the potential policy statements concerned with the change. The negotiation will involve the identification of tactics suitable for the school wishing to implement the plan. These can then be committed to paper by the head who will be responsible for seeing the programme through to its completion. In helping the school

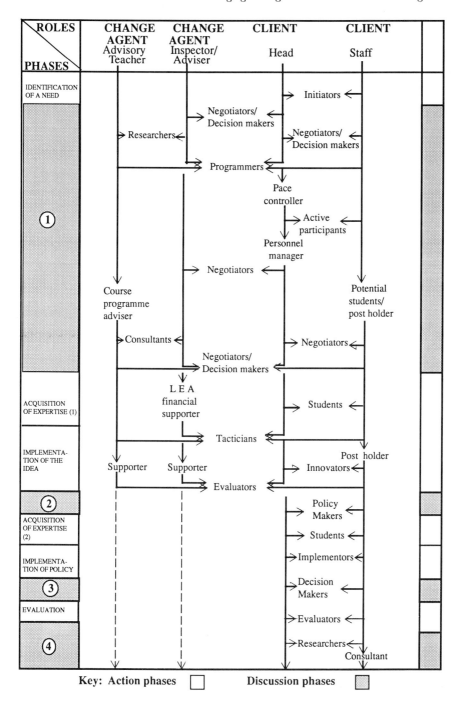

Figure 6.9: The Roles of those Involved in the Application of the Development Framework

acquire the necessary expertise, the role of the curriculum coordinator or advisory teacher is to determine appropriate in-service education. An additional role, in conjunction with the inspector/adviser, is to seek out individual teachers as potential students for more substantial courses. As an alternative, existing expertise in the school can be tapped, either by creating areas of responsibility or re-negotiating existing expertise to accommodate a different approach to the curriculum area under consideration. When negotiations between all parties have been successfully completed and an appropriate course of action has been agreed, an approach may need to be made to the LEA for financial assistance, particularly if a period of secondment is involved.

If the implementation of decisions made in Discussion Phase 1 does involve the acquisition of expertise by staff, individuals will now take on the role of student. This action phase may well occur either in parallel to or in sequence with first level school-based training. During this training, new ideas must be tried out by the teachers in the classroom (School Trial 1), the role now played by the head and staff being that of innovators. While teachers are involved in this 'trial' stage, often, because of the unfamiliarity of the situation, they lose confidence. The change agents must be quick to recognize this occurrence and be ready to play a supportive role. During this innovatory stage, it may become apparent, through an assessment of pupil performance, that some of the original ideas need to be modified. Sufficient time should be allowed for this process to take place. The *Match and Mismatch* in-service package devised by Wynn Harlen for the Schools Council has proved very useful at this stage.

Having tried things out practically in the classroom, it is now possible for the head and staff to embark upon a discussion which will ultimately lead to the formulation of a policy (Discussion Phase 2). The advantage to the school of developing the policy gradually is that the statements made are generalizations based on formally evaluated classroom practice. It must be recognized however, that such generalizations will be most relevant to those involved in their conception and subsequent development. Experience has shown that once teachers have come to terms with the different role, that of a policy maker, their enthusiasm must be fed by the provision of appropriate resources. Also, it is advisable at this stage for those concerned with spreading the innovation, to think in terms of setting-up a coordinated network of like-minded people. This role could be taken on by any one of the four groups concerned. Once the formulation of the policy phase is reached, the outside consultants should be free to begin to work with other schools who wish to embark on a similar change process.

Effective implementation of the new policy only follows when the school comes to terms with the commitment to a problem solving approach to the curriculum, involving continuous monitoring and improvement of practice. This can be achieved by refining the process (Discussion and Action Phase 3). Only when everyone has a common vocabulary and experience is it possible to enter into a consideration of evaluation issues.

The final action phase is evaluation of the policy statements. In making further plans, additional criteria for appraisal should be drawn up, if necessary, by negotiation with the change agents (Discussion Phase 4). It is extremely valuable, at this stage, if the teachers involved acquire the skills of analysis which makes it possible for them to become 'teacher researchers', the post holder taking on the role of change agent in place of the inspector/adviser or advisory teacher. As indicated earlier when such a permanent role change has occurred for the majority of staff of a school, the development of the curriculum can be said to be truly dynamic.

Chapter 7

The Management of Change Within an LEA

Introduction

When considering the management of change within a school, the importance of formulating a policy for change with an in-built strategy for implementation, administration and evaluation, has been stressed. This is none the less important for the management of change within an LEA.

The County Policy for Change

This is outlined below:

1   To provide a means of identifying particular needs on a county-wide basis.

    Appropriate channels of communication need to be set up which are known throughout the county. They rely upon individual teachers, headteachers, advisory teachers, inspectors and advisers knowing who to contact in order that an appropriately planned response, may be made. It is crucial here that requests are channelled through to one person so that development may be seen within the county as a whole.

2   To provide a school focused framework within which curriculum development can operate in the long term.

    Schools are encouraged to adopt a school wide policy for change set against an individual time scale. To help them achieve this, the flexible curriculum development framework described earlier is applied to the school. This has been operating successfully over a ten year period, in a number of Bedfordshire schools. The framework was initially designed to help develop primary science but its use has been extended recently in order to develop the design technology curriculum. The framework involves the school or group of schools in progressing systematically through a number of discussion and action phases according to need, in order to arrive at a series of school policy statements. Schools may enter the framework at a point which is relevant to their stage of development, and progress from one point to another is achieved by selecting and using appropriate tactics in school focused INSET situations using a problem solving approach.

3   To provide a means of meeting need on a county-wide basis both in the long and the short term.

In the short term, schools need support to help them embark upon the process of implementing the National Curriculum. In the long term, support is required to help them 'institutionalize' the necessary change. This requires funding for and access to a variety of INSET, both school and centrally-based. Of significance here in providing a means by which teachers can acquire the necessary expertise, is the notion that quality is more important than quantity and that ongoing professional development activities ideally require the teaching of teachers by teachers so that the work is based firmly upon classroom experiences.

Further support to schools involved in the change process is the provision of a consultancy service which relies heavily on the expertise made available through an advisory teacher team who also implement the INSET programme. In addition to this and the help that can be provided by other external agencies, the value attached to local groups set up to promote liaison and curriculum continuity is of increasing importance. Careful planning, on the part of the LEA, can ensure the setting up of mutual support systems which have an extremely important role to play in the implementation of change within a small geographical area.

An important factor in bringing about change in individual schools or groups of schools is the need to make appropriate resources available to teachers when they are required.

4. To provide an administrative network which allows policy to be implemented effectively.

Schools involved in the process of change need a supportive, administrative network which recognizes the reasons for change and works well to provide for it. When the new arrangement for the local management of schools (LMS) is in place, the need for an LEA to support the developmental process in schools will be just as great; the role of the LEA may be modified as more responsibilities become devolved to schools, but the network will still need to exist.

Decisions made by the members concerning the allocation of resources need to be implemented creatively by professional administrative officers in collaboration with those more closely involved with school-based initiatives leading to the improvement of the school as a whole. Everyone, working inside a school or external to it, will need to know that the network exists and how it can be used effectively to provide for the necessary developments to take place.

5. To monitor and evaluate the success of the development.

Effective monitoring of the change process, in both the short and the long term, requires that evaluation should not only be concerned with summative assessment of progress, but must also include a formative element. Similarly both qualitative and quantitative statements are essential because of their interaction. Such evaluation will not only establish the amount of change taking place in the county as a whole but also, more importantly, it should establish the effectiveness of the change being implemented. The notion that quality is preferable to quantity should be included in the evaluation strategy.

What follows is an attempt to describe the implementation of the policy for change which has been adopted in Bedfordshire. Underpinning the implementation of policy, both in the school and in the LEA, is the need for planning, effective leadership and well thought out administrative strategies.

The Implementation of the County Policy for Change

Needs Identification on a County-Wide Basis

In general terms, Bedfordshire is no different from other LEAs in that the needs identified nationally apply equally well. However, particular schools or groups of schools will have their own individual needs within the overall scenario and, if progress is to be made in the long term, these will have to be known more precisely.

Fairly early on in the development it was necessary for the LEA to make the first approach to schools. Later, when some Bedfordshire schools became aware of the work which was being carried out within the county, they made representations themselves to become involved. In some instances the headteacher would make an approach, and less frequently the whole staff would make a similar appeal. Needless to say, the latter situation was more difficult to deal with but some positive changes were achieved by responding to such demands. Now schools have become much more pro-active in the use of outside assistance and have recognized the value of external support to such an extent that programmes are set up entirely by request. Approaches for individual support can be made through a variety of channels. Heads, sometimes also science and design technology coordinators or class teachers, may make contact with a variety of individuals within the LEA. This being the case, it is important that requests are ultimately managed by one person, the appropriate inspector/adviser, and that headteachers and others know to whom they should be made. Such a simple rule frequently needs reinforcing if schools are not to be disappointed, advisory teachers and others are not to have undue demands made upon them and a county-wide controlled development is to be achieved.

Additionally schools are also in a position to use their own allocation of GRIST funding to buy in outside assistance. In order to be as cost effective as possible, plans are made and submitted jointly by groups of schools arranged in Consortia, as part of a rolling programme. Each Consortium is managed by a senior inspector who also has the ultimate responsibility of approving the requests submitted by the school, in priority order, against a 'needs analysis' for funding which is documented. This information is also made available to the subject-based support teams who are then in a position to respond if it is appropriate to do so. It also serves another very important purpose, that of acting as a record of INSET activity in the county as a whole which can then be used in future planning. A further means of identifying needs is through individual visits by inspectors and advisers and through formal surveys and inspections. Once contact has been made with the school or group of schools and a need for support has been identified, a critical path analysis is applied to the situation (see Figure 7.1)

Initially, past records of involvement, in the form of individual and summary reports kept by the appropriate inspector/adviser, are consulted so that the request is set in a county-wide perspective. This research and subsequent consultation will then lead to a decision being made centrally regarding the most effective use of the support available. For example, it may be desirable to work with only one school or, alternatively, it may be possible for a number of schools with similar needs to be grouped together.

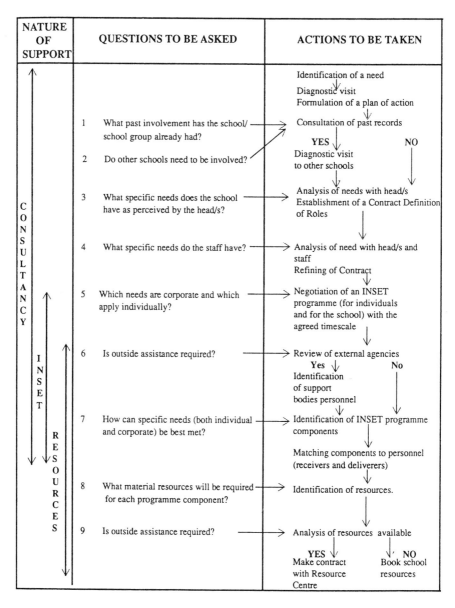

Figure 7.1: Identifying School Needs: A Critical Path Analysis

The initial diagnostic visit, made by the appropriate inspector in order to meet the headteacher/s concerned and identify needs, is crucial in making this decision. Such a visit can also be used to establish that the assistance requested is appropriate in terms of national and county policy and that the needs, as seen by the headteacher/s concerned, are clearly defined so that the right kind of support, agreed by the headteacher/s, is offered by the Authority. At this interview, therefore, a mutually acceptable contract is made with the head of the school or group of schools and a plan of action is formulated. Such long-term planning is fundamental to effective change.

One of the major issues during such interviews is to make sure that the roles and expectations of all concerned are clearly perceived. From the point of view of the LEA it is necessary to establish that all the staff of a school or group of schools are involved in the development. Planning a long time in advance can ensure that this happens provided the leadership within the school is strong. If the reverse is the case, as has happened on occasions in the past, remedial action by the inspector/adviser can be taken against the background of the National Curriculum Statutory Orders. Similarly it must be established that headteachers will be involved in all the planned activities and that they overtly support the development. An issue as simple as the acceptance of an increased noise level whilst developing a practical curriculum is a case in point. It must be made clear to heads that they need to become fully involved and show their appreciation to colleagues who are being brave in trying out something new. The pace of development also needs to be established and agreed. If staff are to be fully involved and the National Curriculum implemented effectively, they must not be pressurized into working at too great a pace. Headteachers need to be sensitive to this point.

After the diagnostic visit, a meeting involving the inspector, the head and appropriate support personnel needs to be arranged to discuss possible developments with the staff of the school. This also serves the covert purpose of identifying the felt needs of individual teachers which could well be quite different to those identified by the head. During this meeting the contract with the school/s is further refined.

Discussion of the kind outlined above can not only identify the need for consultancy or a school-based course but can also reveal the needs of individual staff with regard to centrally based INSET. Individual teachers can be supported on courses which best meet their needs as part of a rolling programme. Of particular importance is the need to select candidates who would benefit from management training, whether this is in terms of leadership within the school or in terms of promoting a particular curricular area. This latter factor has significance in building up areas of expertise within the county which can be 'cascaded' locally using Consortium funding or used to advantage in a pyramid development.

The initial diagnostic and subsequent visits are also valuable in terms of assessing the resource needs of the school. Invariably these needs will emerge during discussion of curriculum matters but, if not, a tour of the school will quickly reveal the true situation. If necessary, the issue of resources can then be raised and confidently discussed in terms of existing knowledge and experience. The following categories of need are commonly identified.

Class teachers may require help in:
Science and design technology education
    Understanding the similarities between science and design technology.
    Understanding the 'process' of science and design technology.
    Their own conceptual understanding.
    Increasing their background knowledge.
    Developing scientific and technological techniques.

Science and design technology teaching skills

Identifying appropriate scientific and technological activities.

Initiating problem solving activities.

Making the work open-ended.

Developing their questioning, observation and listening skills.

Enabling children to record their work appropriately and in different ways.

Employing a variety of teaching styles.

Classroom organization

Organizing practical activities.

Understanding and implementing safety precautions.

Increasing their knowledge of and ability to use resources.

Organizing resources.

Assessment and evaluation

Understanding and using criterion-referenced assessment techniques (eg. Statements of Attainment).

Record keeping.

Developing classroom observational skills.

Evaluating teaching/learning outcomes.

Increasing their self-evaluative skills.

Curriculum planning

Understanding progression.

Matching activities to the needs of individual children so that all have access to the science and design technology curriculum as an entitlement.

Planning for continuity of experience.

Ensuring balance within the science and design technology curriculum.

Integrating science and design technology within the whole curriculum.

Curriculum coordinators usually need help in:

Science and design technology teaching skills

Some of the areas identified in 1 above, according to experience, but often in the categories of assessment and evaluation and curriculum planning.

Middle management skills

Helping class teachers meet the needs identified above.

Defining and implementing their role.

Becoming confident enough to exercise a degree of autonomy.

Developing inter-personal skills with both the head and colleagues.

Resource management

Acquiring, organizing and evaluating resources and equipment.

Developing the school site (inside and outside) for the benefit of science and design technology education.

Communication skills

Keying into the county consultancy network.

Establishing channels of communication within the school.

Headteachers may need help in:

Science and design technology education
> Understanding the science and design technological process.
> Having knowledge of appropriate resources.

Upper management skills
> Developing expertise particularly in group dynamics, time management and interpersonal relationships.
> Defining roles and using staff to best effect using a flexible approach.
> Writing job descriptions and overseeing their operation.
> Using external support creatively.

Managing the National Curriculum
> Formulating and refining National Curriculum Development Plans.
> Planning the overall curriculum to meet the requirements of the National Curriculum.
> Developing and implementing assessment and evaluation procedures along the lines laid down by the National Curriculum.

The School-Focused Framework

This has already been introduced in Chapter 5 and extended in Chapter 6.

Meeting Needs on a County-Wide Basis

In addition to the general needs of schools identified nationally, once the needs of particular schools or groups of schools have been identified as a result of the meetings described above, a decision must be made as to how they may be best met (see Figure 7.1). This step can only be taken with confidence if it is known that a multi-faceted support programme, which can accommodate a whole variety of circumstances, is available both within and out of the county. This frequently relies heavily upon the support of the Bedfordshire Primary Science and Technology Advisory and Support teams, comprised of administrative staff, technicians and advisory teachers who, in turn, are supported by a Cascade team working in schools other than their own for one day per week. The needs identified above may be met both in the long and short term in a variety of ways as shown in Figure 7.2.

If such needs are to be met, this then, as intimated in chapters 5 and 6, presupposes that provision exists for an effective programme of awareness raising training days, school-based INSET, INSET which is available centrally, appropriate resource provision and an efficient consultancy service.

Awareness-raising Training Days

These are provided for both headteachers and curriculum coordinators. The rationale for the training is that having raised awareness of the issues involved and given sufficient guidance on the management side, the materials which have been packaged by the Authority, will be 'cascaded' and further developed in individual schools or groups of

Needs \ Ways in which needs might be met	Short-term programme: Awareness-raising training days	Long term programme: School based courses and team teaching	Long term programme: Centrally based courses	Long term programme: Resource provision	Long term programme: Consultancy
Science technology education		✓	✓	✓	
Science technology teaching skills		✓	✓	✓	
Classroom organization		✓	✓		
Assessment and evaluation	✓	✓	✓		✓
Curriculum planning	✓	✓	✓	✓	✓
Resource management		✓	✓	✓	✓
Communication skills			✓		✓
Middle management skills	✓		✓		✓
Upper management skills	✓		✓		✓
Managing the National Curriculum	✓	✓	✓	✓	✓

Figure 7.2: Meeting Needs on a County Wide Basis

schools on a 'self help' basis. Such a system is the only way in which all schools within an authority can be reached in time to embark upon the implementation of the National Curriculum within the timescale laid down by the government.

Whilst some schools will require little help in addition to this short term programme, others will require substantial help over a much longer period, the kind of support which only a longer term programme can provide.

School-based INSET

Over a period of time, the systematic approach applied to the management of the change process has caused a build up of demand for school-based support from schools until at the present time the planned programme of involvement stretches far into the future. The implications as such mean that a well defined programme of courses and long term support must be planned in order to maximize the efficient use of personnel and resources. Examples of typical responses are given in chapter 6.

There are a variety of ways in which this can be achieved. Once the request has been channelled to the appropriate person, it can be considered in terms of development within the country as a whole. Frequently, with small schools, the request is a joint one coming from a group who have already made contact with each other for another purpose. However, if one or two small schools in a larger group indicate that they require help, then the remaining schools will actually be canvassed to join. Involvement in the same in-service experience may well lead to a form of communication network being set up. Once the network is set up, communication links allow a real exchange of ideas to take place and a common ground established from which natural progression from one group of schools to another is possible. However, this situation needs to be handled carefully since it may well be that the stages of development of the two sub-groups are too far apart for the liaison to be profitable. In this case, both sub-groups would still be given the opportunity to be involved, but perhaps separately, so that the performance gap within the larger group is narrowed rather than widened. Alternatively, a differentiated programme can be offered but care must be taken to ensure that the programme is meaningful to the individual teachers involved as well as fulfilling the needs of each institution.

Working in this way enables schools to begin to support each other and opens up opportunities for liaison not only in science and design technology but also in other areas of the curriculum. Experience has shown, however, that the needs of individual schools co-operating as a group cannot be matched so closely as those schools being supported as a single institution. More time and effort will be needed in any initial planning and subsequent implementation before much development can be expected. This is inevitable since individual teachers, meeting together from a number of schools, need time to overcome the understandable initial shyness which will exist in the larger group. A longer period of time may be necessary before any real progress is made, as there will almost certainly be a need to build up the confidence of the group before they may be willing to reveal their true needs. However, with the application of a certain amount of skill and patience, the outcome can be very rewarding. Time must be spent on activities which enable those involved to begin to get to know one another well. It is only in this way that any barriers to successful professional communication can be lowered sufficiently for the necessary trust to be established within the group. The course leaders must be sufficiently sensitive to the needs of the group to provide a coherent programme which allows for individuals within it to progress in their own terms.

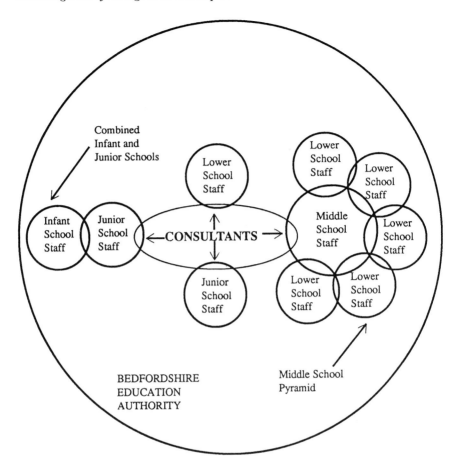

Figure 7.3: Types of School-focused Initiative

In the case of a single school, large or small, the response to needs can be targeted precisely. It is necessary to consider a number of factors before becoming committed to a particular programme. Of prime importance is the profile of the group of staff concerned; the expectations and leadership style of the headteacher; the pupils in the catchment area from which they are drawn; the expectations of parents and the influence of the governing body. Provided the needs and the feel of a single school situation have been assessed reasonably well, then success can be assured.

Although, in spite of the overwhelming demand, no one school has been turned down, it has been necessary to take care that requests are not taken in isolation. Figure 7.3 summarizes the variety of working groups which are operating in Bedfordshire. The pattern of the grouping of schools may be such that one Infant School, for the purposes of in-service, joins with its neighbouring Junior School or a number of Lower Schools link up with the Middle School to which their pupils transfer. Alternatively, it may be necessary to work with one school in isolation and then the establishment of a network similar to that described above is more difficult to achieve. Most groupings are based on established pyramids of schools and reflect the route along which individual children progress. In some instances it has been possible to involve a third tier (the Upper School) in the liaison group and this has tremendous implications for the consideration of continuity, progression and curricular balance. In areas of dense population, however, geographical proximity has been the basis upon which schools have been grouped and care has been taken to try to involve all schools in the area even if this means working with a number of large schools on an individual basis. Thus, with careful management, feeder schools can be brought closer together with respect to their level of development and, as a consequence, continuity of experience for individual children has a greater chance of being established.

Once the needs of a school or group of schools have been put into perspective with regard to the county as a whole, a mutually acceptable contract has been made with those involved and a plan of action has been agreed, management responsibilities are transferred to the advisory teacher who will lead the development along the lines described in chapter 6. He or she is now expected to implement the programme in conjunction with the school and liaise with the headteacher. However, close communication with the inspector is expected, particularly when progress becomes problematic and a joint decision regarding the way forward has to be made. Great care must be taken not to undermine the authority of the advisory teacher and only in extreme cases of difficulty should it be necessary for the inspector to intervene. Even then, the advisory teacher should be involved and be fully in agreement with the steps which are proposed.

Frequently, due to a lack of human resources, a direct response to a request for development cannot be made quickly. Since it is a policy to continue to support the establishment of a long term contract for a school, which enables the changes which have taken place within the school to remain when the external support is withdrawn, the original way of working must remain unaltered in terms of an overall framework. Nevertheless, some responses to urgent requests for help need to be made. In these cases, arrangements allow for a short term response to be made through 'training days' and a limited school-based INSET programme so that a start may be made prior to the establishment of a longer term and more intensive commitment.

Centrally-based INSET

In the past, alongside this school-based programme, a crucial ingredient in the implementation of change strategies in individual schools has been the policy to make centrally-based courses available to teachers. These focus not only on science and design technology education but also on the management of curriculum change; both have been targeted at a number of levels to provide for the progression and development of individual teachers.

Indeed, in some schools, progress towards the main aim of implementing a changed science and design technology curriculum may well be slowed down because those involved may need to acquire further expertise by attending long or short courses. It may be no bad thing in some instances, if the school-based development is preceded by individuals attending courses which are designed to help with the change process. Bedfordshire, along with a number of other LEAs, supports activities and courses at local and regional level and actively seeks to strengthen this provision using GRIST funding. In this way, teachers are able to increase their expertise in science and design technology as well as develop their management skills in order to implement change.

Courses need to be provided in both school and curriculum management of science and design technology so that teachers can progress in their thinking and practice. Experience has shown that the provision of expertise in the subject area only is insufficient and that more rapid progress can be made if the two aspects, the subject and management, are dealt with in parallel. It is important that each school subscribes to the notion of a developmental structure for INSET and ensures all teachers are fully aware of the progress achieved at a particular point in time.

Increasingly centrally-based INSET is designed in such a way that participants are required to enter into a contract which will ensure that they will use their expertise for the benefit of others after the course has finished. Some of this expertise can be more formally used to set up 'cascade' teams so that further dissemination of the implementation process takes place at a local level. Gradually schools learn to use the bank of recognized expertise to support their school-based in-service requirements which can now be funded under GRIST Consortium arrangements.

Resourcing County-wide

An important factor in bringing about change in schools is the need to make clear to teachers what it is that needs to be changed. This is particularly relevant to the nature and use of resources.

The clerical and technical support team based at the Centre play a vital role in supporting all courses staffed by the advisory teacher team. The materials required are of two kinds, those required to implement workshops with teachers and those needed to support professional development through the team teaching of topic work with children.

Over the years it has been policy to develop and trial a variety of workshops which can be used in either school or centrally-based situations. A selection of these workshops is included in Part 2. Indeed the success of the course work in Bedfordshire has been largely due to the existence of materials which allowed an instant response to be made to an identified need. The list of contents in Part II illustrates the variety of materials available for use. Each workshop, with a guide for participants and tutors, can be implemented in about sixty to ninety minutes. Some require feedback from the classroom and all rely heavily on the personal teaching experiences of participants. In addition, many of the workshops require AVA materials and equipment of various kinds and these have been packaged in a motivating manner by the support teams.

The production and refinement of materials for topic work with children has also taken place over a number of years. When a member of the advisory team is working in a school, it is important that the materials used maximize the development of science and design technology within the class. With this in mind, and, also, to deflect the burden of resourcing from the teacher, a number of suitable topics have been developed so that, for each, a series of activities are available for three to four children. The activities are boxed and each consists of a pupil workcard, a teacher's guide and the materials required to carry out the work. Whilst it is accepted that from day to day, science does not 'come in boxes', this has been found to be a very convenient way of resourcing schools for the purposes of school-based work. Furthermore, for schools with adequate storage facilities, or for those which have developed a central science and design technology resource area, contents lists have been computerized so that they can be passed on to schools who wish to resource activities for themselves.

In addition, all Bedfordshire primary and middle schools are entitled to borrow resources from the Centre. Books, animals, AVA materials, some licensed computer software, hardware of various kinds, equipment, tools and boxed multi-media materials of the kind described above are all available for loan. Recently, a major growth area has been to replicate popular materials (up to five sets of topic areas are held in stock) and increase the variety of materials available for study. This has already had a major impact on the work in schools and will continue to be a priority, especially in relation to National Curriculum Attainment Targets. Even so, materials are in such great demand that most schools find it necessary to book them at least a term in advance, which has had a beneficial effect on curriculum planning. However, the specific aim of this loan service is to raise the awareness of teachers to what is required to implement effectively the science and design technology curriculum in school. The need to book ahead puts pressure upon schools to resource themselves; help in achieving this goal is readily available from the Centre.

To support this idea a number of 'exemplar' kits are also available for loan. These may cover general items (class kit and school kit) or may be more specific (colour and light kit, electricity kit etc). Each consists of a number of recommended items in the area concerned, together with a list of prices and addresses of suppliers. Schools may borrow a kit for a period of time, try out the equipment and decide which to buy when finance permits. This prevents schools selecting from the catalogue and running the risk of buying a 'pig in a poke' which only partly fits the needs of the pupils.

As mentioned above, it is policy that schools put a rolling programme in operation which allows them to eventually resource themselves. For some schools, however, the basic cost of equipment precludes this possibility. Early on, schools motivated to include design technology within the curriculum were having difficulty in finding sufficient resources to provide basic tool and construction kits for the children to use. Support, provided by the Authority on a fifty-fifty funding basis, enabled just under half of Bedfordshire Primary Schools to acquire such equipment and this one move has had a marked effect on the introduction of this area of the curriculum. Further welcome support, also on a fifty-fifty basis for the rest of the schools, was made the following year. Also a technology trolley, designed by a member of the advisory team and manufactured by the Bedfordshire Technology Unit of the Teaching Media Resource Service, is currently on trial in schools.

In addition, Consortium funding has allowed an increasing number of schools to support staff on a Science and Technology Centre visit. This type of visit is often used as a preliminary to a school-based course and raises the awareness of teachers not only to what is available but also, through the medium of display, to show how materials have been used in schools. Currently, for these visits, the demand is so great that it has been necessary to establish a system of booking in order that time may be used efficiently. Also, to support the visits, an information booklet has been produced.

Another major growth area is in the field of publications. Although there are a number of commercially produced schemes available to teachers, there has been a real need for the production of appropriate, open-ended materials in certain areas and age ranges. To meet this need, the Primary Science and Technology Team has researched, trialled and published a number of curriculum materials. Details are given in the reference section. Although, initially, each publication was developed by a particular member of the project team, it is now customary to fund a team of teachers to develop the work. Brainstorming by such a group can produce a wealth of ideas which can be further refined prior to publication. Another positive feature of such publications is that photographs of local situations and schools can be included so that they are more motivating to Bedfordshire teachers. Currently, publications are now being linked firmly to the requirements of the National Curriculum Attainment Targets.

Another feature, concerned with publications, is the production of local AVA materials for use with workshops. The visual presentation of the change process being implemented already by some schools in the county, adds strength to that process when it is being advocated to other schools. Using the county photographer, together with a member of the support team, a bank of local photographs illustrating a variety of aspects of science and design technology education has been set up. Similarly, video material illustrating a variety of classroom situations has been produced.

Consultancy, Public Relations and Liaison

A large part of the work with the team is concerned with consultancy. The advisory teacher team concern themselves with curriculum matters such as the use of computers, advice on appropriate teacher/pupil materials, classroom management, the building up of appropriate resource bases and the use of the school site. This work complements and supports that of the inspector who has a monitoring role, particularly in relation to the management of the school, assessment and delivery of the curriculum in relation to national priorities. Contact, by the school, can be established, by telephone or through working with the advisory teacher. Alternatively, particular needs can be made known through the County Inspector who then responds to the request in an appropriate way.

However, the support team also play an important part where resources are concerned. Advice on particular items can be provided at the Centre or the appropriate technician can visit a school and provide assistance on the use of specific resources. This is particularly important when matters of safety are concerned.

Another important aspect of the work of the advisory and support teams is in the field of public relations and liaison with schools. When schools are in the process of introducing new ways of working, it is important that others, close to the school, understand what is involved. When steps are taken to achieve this relationship, the development of the school curriculum is more likely to take place.

Effective liaison is particularly important at the primary/secondary interface if curriculum continuity is to be preserved. Every opportunity must be taken to raise the awareness of teachers to what has been achieved previously, not only in order to support progression, but also to ensure that pupils' former achievements are not underestimated. Where school-focused professional development has taken place, the opportunity for liaison is built in to the programme itself. In schools not so involved, liaison has been less easily achieved but the use of Consortium funding to support visits to other schools and/or liaison meetings is increasing.

The involvement of industry is also an important issue. At primary level, discussion has already taken place between the Luton Chamber of Commerce and its associated 'Industry Matters Committee'. As a result, a closer liaison has been established with industry and there is a good understanding of the initiatives which are being undertaken in schools. Arrangements for 'shadowing' experiences are currently underway and a programme of workshop-based meetings involving teachers and leading local industrialists is being implemented on a regular basis. Both industrial and school venues are used. If work in primary schools is to be made relevant to youngsters, it is crucial that links with industry are exploited. In the past the main problem has been the lack of awareness on the part of local companies to the needs of primary schools together with a lack of understanding that attitudes are formed very early on in a child's life. It is too late to leave this awareness raising to the secondary phase. Recent experience has shown that now company directors are better informed about primary education, they are very willing to go out of their way to forge links with schools. This is a major breakthrough into a world that has to be cost effective and thus has to consider very carefully the value to the company of a visit by a primary school.

Most important of all is the involvement of parents and governors. On a number of occasions, parents, governors and children of particular primary schools have been given the opportunity to be actively engaged in science and design technology activities. The purpose has been to allow those involved to enjoy and understand a problem solving approach to teaching and learning. A modification of this approach has also taken place in a multi-cultural context. The children were engaged in a practical activity whilst the parents, guided by a broadsheet translated into their first language, were given the opportunity to discuss the work with their own children.

The Provision of an Administrative Network

Whatever the desired development might be in terms of school improvement, it will need to be supported by an administrative communications network which fully appreciates the need for change. The curriculum development process is likely to be initiated by the members of an inspection/advisory service. Through the regular monitoring of the stages of development reached by individual schools, inspectors and advisers are in a good position to assess the advisory support which needs to be applied at any one time. A team of subject advisers, suitably qualified and trained into the role of advisory teacher, are essential if the required curriculum support is to be provided to schools. It is also essential that through the early stages of the implementation of the National Curriculum in schools, the inspectorial and advisory function is maintained as one coherent process, even though the two separate functions may be carried out by different people. Also, as time goes by, it may be necessary for the LEA to reassess the balance between the monitoring and support needed by schools in the county as a whole.

In Bedfordshire, the Science and Technology Centre, which now acts as the base for the advisory team, was set up by the Authority long before central resource support was made available, through the ESG project, as it was already recognized that the development of a practical area of the curriculum, like science and design technology, will need to provide ready access for teachers to apparatus, equipment, materials and reference books.

Targeted funding provided by Central Government allowed the LEA to appoint more staff to enhance the developments in schools and cause them to take place more rapidly. These developments were speeded up further by the arrangement introduced in 1987 for Grant Related In-service Training Funding (GRIST). The possibility of more appointments, usually on a fixed term basis of advisory teachers, the secondment on a part-time basis of teachers to acquire expertise and more importantly the devolution of some funding to schools to support their own school-based in-service training, made the circle of support complete. With such arrangements in existence, few schools have the excuse not to participate in activities designed to develop the curriculum and improve standards and opportunities for the children involved.

It must be recognized that the targeted support supplied by central government was incomplete and for 'pump priming' only, the additional funding being supplied by the LEA. The resources allocated to projects such as the development of science and design technology in the primary school were then overseen by the professional administrative officers of the Authority. The need for a good communications network between all the parties involved should now be clearly seen. In fact, the network, to be complete, should also enhance departments other than education, who will have an involvement from time to time.

The changes in the classroom experiences needed for children to prepare them for the very different world in which they will live can only be provided effectively through a flexible administrative network of people who understand and who are committed to fulfilling such needs. Teams of advisory teachers have been set up to advise and implement the changes necessary to comply with the National Curriculum. The leader of such a subject team will almost certainly be an adviser or an inspector who will need to be supplied with information so that he/she can effectively fulfil the role of coordinator on a county-wide basis. In terms of the development of an inspection/advisory service, this curriculum team management role is relatively new. Recognition of such a role must be made if uniform standards of development are to be achieved throughout an LEA.

Figure 7.4 is an attempt to summarize the ways in which the advisory teacher team and school coordinators interact to bring about school improvement. The advisory teacher can take on one or more of several roles. First, they can act as trainers of classroom teachers and school coordinators, on centrally-based courses, with the expectation that each co-ordinator will return to school to lead curriculum development. Second, they themselves might take on the role of curriculum development leader within a school or school group. The third role, which they most certainly always take on, is that of advisory or support teacher within a school or school group. This involves providing support in the form of team teaching and being available to offer advice. Back at the Centre, they take on the role of consultant, responding to the many and various enquiries and requests coming in by the telephone. Some of these may be dealt with immediately, whilst others require a visit to the school concerned. They also have an important role to play as material producers, developing new pupil teacher resources according to need. Some productions are published locally whilst others are promoted on a national scale. Lastly, they are also responsible for acquiring and cataloguing the additional resources necessary to implement the National Curriculum.

The Management of the Primary Science and Technology Team

Managing a team of people working centrally within an LEA, advising and supporting the change process, is similar to the management of a team of teachers employed in a school. It is vital that the roles of individuals and subgroups within the team are clearly defined and perceived. Furthermore, role definition must follow closely the expertise that is currently available within the team with sufficient flexibility introduced to allow for maximization of expertise and changing roles should this be advantageous and necessary.

Of prime importance is the need for an effective support team, without whom the advisory team could not function. At a simplistic level the technical side of the Bedfordshire team takes care of the resource implications whilst the administrative branch deals with the clerical aspects and the documentation required. In practice, the situation is not so straightforward. Two of the three technicians have word processing and management skills which they develop creatively according to need, whilst the third exercises her ability to relate to people in dealing with the school loan service. The clerical assistant is an audio

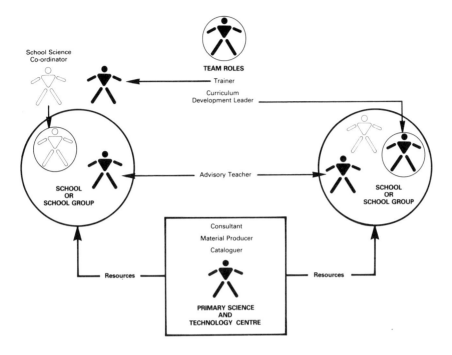

Figure 7.4: The Varied Role of an Advisory Teacher in Relation to the School Coordinator

typist who can also use a word processor. Additionally she is a trained photographer and is invaluable in producing publicity material and resources used by schools and the Centre. She is also more than capable of taking on the role of technician should this be required. The secretary, who is a copy typist, has learned to manage the multi-media loan system with great efficiency. She has also had to develop interpersonal skills in her receptionist/telephonist role together with a knowledge of science and design technology education in providing guided tours of the Centre for teacher groups and others.

The work of the advisory team is clearly to do with consultancy, research, the production of support materials and INSET, both school and centrally-based. However, each of the three full-time advisory teachers and ten part-time cascaders have different strengths to offer. Collectively the whole team has expertise, over a 3–13 age range, in science, design and technology, computer control, multicultural and special education. Additionally, one advisory teacher manages the cascade team who support the advisory teachers.

From what has been said hitherto, it must be obvious that all members of the team have been chosen not only for the particular expertise which they have to offer but also for their ability to adapt, work with others and utilize their strengths according to need. To recruit personnel with the appropriate personalities is often far more important in the implementation of change strategies on a team basis, than to recruit those with rather narrow, predetermined qualifications.

In managing the team, the county inspector designs each advisory teacher's programme and, because each is very highly motivated to take on all aspects of the job, great care needs to be taken to ensure that insurmountable central demands are not put upon individuals. The work has to be very carefully structured and, to save travelling time, advisory teachers are allocated schools on a geographical basis. Time must be allocated for team building activities, material production, research and INSET as well as for work in schools. Of these, the team building time is particularly important. Much value can be gained from regularly working together, often informally, to plan ahead, exchange ideas, discuss strategies and reflect upon the work in hand. In striving to be accountable, it is all too tempting for the manager to plan for the whole week to be devoted to work in schools. Managers need to resist this temptation and plan for the effective use of team time.

The current level of work has resulted from an evaluation of past programmes and is in line with the directed time available for use. A diary is kept for each member, time for activities other than school-based work being deliberately set aside from the outset, including a certain amount of space for trouble shooting. Dates for the school-based course session can then be entered in the diary at the diagnostic interview with the headteacher, after a time scale for the initiative has been agreed. The number of teachers in the group often determines the length of course, since sufficient time needs to be set aside for the team teaching element. With large groups, even with the support of one or two cascaders, three terms is the norm. With small schools it is important that the time scale is not over-condensed. Teachers need time to try out new ideas and reflect upon different approaches to learning, and experience has shown that at least two terms need to be set aside to allow this to happen. Bringing about curriculum development most often involves changing attitudes and it is important that the external change agent, the advisory teacher, does not withdraw too early allowing the situation to 'refreeze' to that which existed in the past.

Having agreed to the time scale, the frequency and pattern of the after school course sessions needs to be discussed. For initiatives with a technological bias, it is often useful to bunch several sessions together at the outset, say on a weekly or fortnightly basis, so that familiarization with techniques can be acquired. For others, the sessions might need to be more evenly spaced. Certainly it is not necessary to be specific at this stage about the focus of each session. Needs will be revealed as teachers begin to involve their children in science and design technology activity: the content can be negotiated with the advisory teacher in the light of their experiences. Each advisory teacher is also responsible for booking team teaching once adequate space has been allocated in the programme. This is also entered in the diary which then becomes an important document, invaluable as an evaluative tool but also useful for the purposes of accountability.

The programme of work for the support team also needs to be carefully managed if undue demands are not to be placed upon them. Although time can be set aside on a weekly basis for routine tasks such as processing loans, assessing new materials and so on, a good deal of the work cannot be planned in advance. Obviously, part of their programme is determined by the work of the advisory team but, additionally, all Bedfordshire primary schools have open access to the Centre. A further complication is that the work load peaks, particularly at the beginning and end of term. Planning, in this situation, has to involve building in mechanisms which not only enable each member of the team to prioritize her particular work load but also to put that to one side in order to make a team response during peak periods. This way of working demands great flexibility and skills in management on the part of those involved. It also requires the establishment of a communication network through which responses can be made immediately. One way that this has been achieved has been through the use of booking forms for rooms, for course materials and for typing. The first two have to be submitted an agreed time in advance while the latter is produced in three different colours to indicate urgency which has helped enormously in allowing individuals to prioritize. (However, such a system can only work if all the people concerned trust and respect each other to the extent that undue demands are not made upon them and that it is acceptable to say 'no'.) Another way, particularly in dealing with peak periods, has been through meetings specifically designed to allow a whole team approach to solving the problem in hand. The solution may well involve some members of the team taking on a new role on a temporary basis. Of considerable help here is the development of flow diagrams illustrating particular processes, for example, the steps required to access a new item or to accept the return of a school loan. Obviously this information is invaluable when there are changes in staffing.

It is already obvious that the smooth running of the team relies heavily on the establishment of good internal channels of communication, both formal and informal. To this end, one day per week is set aside for meetings of various kinds. Although a degree of flexibility has to be allowed, an advisory team meeting is held on a weekly basis, four meetings per term usually being set aside for a whole team approach involving the support team. All members of the team are invited to contribute to the agenda but a degree of planning has to take place to ensure that there is enough time for discussion of major issues. The focus of such meetings can be planning, information exchange, curriculum, current issues or evaluation. A formal agenda is produced and notes of the meeting are taken as a record of decisions made. Although final decisions are the responsibility of the inspector leading the team, the exchange of ideas and brainstorming which can take place in such a forum are invaluable, not only in the development of the work but also in the management of the project. Having a whole day set aside also allows for other meetings to take place. These are mainly concerned with planning and are set up on an informal basis. In connection with the support team, the recognition by the advisory team that it is acceptable for them to meet on their own, represented very real progress. The fact that such meetings take place on a regular basis means that problems can be dealt with quickly, minor decisions implemented immediately and ownership of the work is ensured.

When all the team are present in the office, however, care must be taken that an individual's time is not wasted. It is too easy to seek personal attention over matters which can more easily and efficiently be dealt with on paper. It is worth taking some time in establishing the use of internal memos for this purpose together with the idea that separate issues require separate memos. This facilitates making a response and also aids in filing. Other forms of documentation are also necessary. Notes of the inspector's diagnostic and follow-up visits are made and passed on to the advisory teacher who will lead the development. Similarly each advisory teacher makes a termly report of his or her work in school. The nature of the workshops and team teaching is recorded and this is then available as an invaluable record when a school wishes to begin second level training.

Communication with others, outside the team, is also important. Termly meetings are held with the senior inspectors, both for the purpose of reporting progress and pre-planning the school-based work. Termly reports are also passed on to the senior inspectors and other appropriate advisers/inspectors for information purposes. Individual advisory teachers also represent the team on a variety of outside bodies such as the London Zoo, the School Library Service and so on. Reports of meetings, as are reports of other visits, are documented but can also be given individually at a team meeting. Here it is important to make sure that such reports do not become an unnecessary burden and with this in mind, a special form, designed by the team members, is used.

Another very important facet of management is planning for the professional development of each team member on an annual basis. This starts with the confidential professional development interview which relies on a series of questions about the work environment known to the interviewee before-hand. Although opportunity is given for discussion of any relevant issue, the questions serve to focus the mind and 'break the ice'. Experience has shown that, if this occasion is handled sensitively, much useful information can be gained and used not only to help the individual concerned but also to benefit the team. An example of how this works follows. An advisory teacher expressed a desire to attend a particular course and this was arranged. Not only did she gain from the experience but also arrangements were made for her to pass on the expertise to others through 'in-house' INSET. Furthermore, a desire, expressed at interview, to use her photographic skills has enabled the clerical assistant to also take on the role of team photographer.

Once needs are known it is important that some follow-up takes place. A certain amount of funding needs to be made available in advance so that some team members can attend out-of-county courses as part of a rolling programme. Of equal importance is the need to set aside some time for an 'in-house' course programme, usually at the beginning and/or end of term. As mentioned previously, individuals in the team brought different strengths with them and these have been added to through attendance at national courses; the 'in-house' course allows this expertise to be 'cascaded' to others in the team. It should also be said that this facility is as valuable to the support team as it is to the advisory teachers, and day sessions can be profitably run for the whole team. This not only serves as a team building exercise, but also gives individuals an insight into other aspects of the work. With this in mind, regular visits to schools for the support team are also arranged and paired advisory teacher visits are encouraged for the purposes of widening experience. Thus an advisory teacher recruited from a middle school craft, design and technology department is now able to teach science effectively in a reception class on a regular basis and without getting paint all over his clothes!

Discussion on the management of a large team (eleven full-time equivalent teachers) would not be complete without an evaluative element. Although major faults in the system are easy to spot, areas needing less drastic improvement are more difficult to identify. A crucial factor here is in building up sufficient confidence within the team that difficulties can be openly discussed without offence being taken. The difficult task of admitting one's mistakes has to be overcome and the need to rethink ways of working, in the light of new circumstances, accepted. Knowing when to intervene and when to leave well alone has to be learned. The provision of a framework which is flexible, which seeks opinion and which encourages people to express their views is crucial to success. Above all, it is necessary not only to set sufficient time aside for management purposes but also to learn to manage that time efficiently. Effective time management has to be achieved if leadership of the team is to succeed.

The Evaluation of the Initiative

There are two major facets to evaluation which are of interest to an LEA. These are the monitoring of the effectiveness of LEA support and the cost effectiveness of the management framework adopted.

Aspect	Formative evaluation	Summative evaluation

Qualitative evaluation	1. Working groups
	   1.1 The science and technology working party
	   1.2 The primary working party
	   1.3 The primary science and technology project management groups
	   1.4 Meetings with Senior Inspectors
		1. Project progress statement

	2. Termly reports from Advisory Teachers	2. Letters from headteachers
	3. Inspectors 'After Care' Programme	3. INSET Analysis
Quantitative evaluation	4. GRIST: Primary needs analysis	4. School-based course record
	5. Advanced bookings	5. Teachers' Questionnaire 6. Adviser's/Inspector's evaluative visits

Figure 7.5: Aspects of the Evaluation of the Development of Primary Science and Design Technology in Bedfordshire

The Monitoring of the Effectiveness of LEA Support

Monitoring progress in the LEA is an important process in establishing the effectiveness of the support offered. Aspects of formative evaluation, shown in Figure 7.5, have been included as follows:

1   Working groups provide a forum for the exchange of ideas, analysis of needs as perceived by teachers and appraisal of current initiatives. The frequency with which the groups meet determines the rate at which particular responses can be made; in urgent cases, however, the matter is usually dealt with through personal contact between those needing to be involved.

2   Termly reports from the advisory teachers and members of the cascade team are also used. By their nature, these are subjective, but do serve as a self-evaluation tool for the advisory teacher concerned, facilitate the comparison of schools in which he or she works and alert the county inspector to schools where a more intensive 'after care' programme is required. These reports are circulated to the Middle and Primary Phase inspectors, advisers/inspectors for science and design technology and senior inspectors.

3   The inspector's 'after care' programme is also used diagnostically. On the withdrawal of the advisory teacher from a school or group of schools and after a short period of time has elapsed, the inspector re-establishes contact with the school in

Academic year	School-based curriculum development			Management training centre				Total schools involved
	No. of A.T's working	No. of schools involved	No. of Teachers involved	DPSE technology education	ASE Dip. in science ed. (35 days)	Co-ord Course (35 hours)	Co-ord Conference (2 days)	
Year X	2	41	252	—	6	—	—	50
Year Y	3	83	313	—	5	25	—	103
Year Z prognosis	5	102 (60 new schools already booked)	556 (estimate 300 new teachers)	4 (new schools)	4 (new schools)	10 (new schools)	40 (estimate 20 new schools)	160

Figure 7.6: INSET Analysis: Primary Science and Design Technology

order that support is still seen to be available. In this way, formative monitoring can continue to take place on a regular basis.

4 Under LEA arrangements for the Consortia, schools have been asked to identify their needs with respect to national priority areas, one of these being science and design technology. Responses are collated under the heading of 'GRIST: Primary Needs Analysis' and experience to date has shown that between 60 per cent and 70 per cent of schools express a positive interest in developing the science and design technology curriculum as a priority area.

5 The success of any curriculum development initiative must, surely, also be measured in terms of market demands. The number of advance bookings has been used as a measure of success prior to the 1988 Education Act. At that point in time, bookings for the Bedfordshire team already extended into 1991.

Summative evaluation is also an effective means of measuring progress.

1 Although tedious to produce, annual progress statements are an invaluable means of communicating what has actually been undertaken. Curriculum development is inevitably a slow process and it is all too easy to assume that little has been achieved. Comparison of such progress statements on an annual basis provides positive evidence of development or not, as the case may be.

2 Letters or any forms of communication from headteachers are also invaluable in monitoring effectiveness. Experience has shown that, quite rightly, heads are quick to complain but, more importantly, they are also willing to express their satisfaction with the support which is being offered.

3 When a planned approach to curriculum development is taken on a county-wide basis, it is a relatively simple matter to analyze the number of INSET initiatives which have taken place. A document, similar to the one produced in Figure 7.6, can provide figures concerning the numbers of schools and teachers involved, on an annual basis.

    Similarly, it is also possible to carry out an analysis of the phases of schools involved as follows in Figure 7.7. This is particularly relevant currently, in light of the implementation of the National Curriculum. Also relevant is the identification of particular teachers who have potential, as a result of centrally-based training, to lead developments within their own areas.

4 School-based course records can also be used quantitatively as an evaluative tool. Team members are expected to complete a school-based course record. It not only acts as a course record and a self-evaluative tool for the advisory teacher concerned but also identifies the future needs of particular schools. For example, two team members' perceptions of the results of their interaction with the total sample of twenty-nine schools is recorded on a five point scale in Figure 7.8.

    In addition it was thought that of the twenty-nine schools, six would benefit from an immediate 'after care' programme, whilst six schools had achieved enough impetus to continue under their own momentum. Seventeen schools would possibly be ready for second level training after a period of consolidation.

5 In order to take into account the views of teachers, an anonymous questionnaire is administered at the end of each school-based course (of two to three terms) to schools selected at random. The analysis recorded below represented five schools

submitting thirty-five reply sheets for analysis with respect to the question 'how have you gained?'.

— Thirty-two teachers reported that, in various ways, they had gained in confidence with regard of teaching science and design technology.
— Twenty-five teachers commented that the course had raised their awareness of issues such as skill and concept acquisition, progression and balance, and thus the importance of integrating science and design technology into the whole curriculum.
— Thirteen teachers experienced an attitude change as a result of the course. They became more aware of the importance of problem solving and first-hand experience together with the need for a change in teaching style and the provision of a differentiated curriculum.
— Eight teachers have been able to develop their classroom management skills as a result of the course.

Phase	Total number of schools	Number of schools involved			Total number	Per cent of Schools
		Year X	Year Y	Year Z		
Lower	156	30	46	26	102	65%
Middle	43	5	8	5	18	42%
Infant	34	5	2	3	10	29%
Junior	34	2	8	2	12	35%
Primary	5	0	1	0	1	20%
Total	272	42	65	36	143	53%

(Source G. A. Pennell)

Figure 7.7: An Analysis of a County-wide INSET Initiative.

Advisory Teacher 1:

				Success rate			
Evaluation (12 schools)		High ⟨– – – – – – – – – – – – – –⟩ Low					
Success of the Course Sessions	—		6	4	2		—
Success of the Term Teaching	—		5	5	2		—

Advisory Teacher 2:

				Success rate			
Evaluation (17 schools)		High ⟨– – – – – – – – – – – – – –⟩ Low					
Success of the Course Sessions	—		10	7	—		—
Success of the Term Teaching	1		6	7	3		—

(Source G. A. Pennell)

Figure 7.8: Advisory Teachers' Self Evaluation of their Interaction with a Sample of 29 Schools

It was rewarding that not only had the prime objective of the course, that of building confidence, been achieved in the sample of five schools selected, but also, other objectives important in implementing change, those of raising awareness and changing attitudes, had been effected in a large number of teachers concerned. There was no doubt that the change in strategy employed had been successful in the short term.

6. In the long term, when schools have settled to a natural rhythm of work, a more objective approach to evaluation has been taken. Once an advisory teacher has withdrawn from a school, a formal visit is arranged by the appropriate inspector in order to re-establish contact with the school. After a longer period of time, say perhaps a year, a more meaningful evaluation can take place. At this point schools are presented with an evaluative questionnaire supplemented by interviews of those concerned.

Cost-Effectiveness of the Management Framework Adopted

As indicated earlier, the team teaching element, which enabled class teachers to carry out and evaluate in practice issues which had been discussed in theory in workshop situations, was seen to be vital to the success of the initiative. However, with large schools or clusters it was difficult to respond to all the teachers involved, even over a period of three terms, and it became increasingly clear that more human resources were needed to implement this aspect of the model. In 1986, the decision which Bedfordshire had to make was whether to appoint two additional full-time advisory teachers or ten part-time personnel, each of whom could work alongside the advisory teachers for one day per week, the remaining four days being spent in their own schools. Eventually, it was decided that funding through the ESG scheme should be used to support the secondment of the teachers who would become part of a 'cascade' model of development, the cascade team, as described in an article by Pennell, Petrie and Bent (1989).

The broad intention was that each would then spend his/her 'cascade' day between two schools in complementing the classroom work of the advisory teacher leading the curriculum development. Initially each would work in their own school cluster group in promoting science and design technology whilst, at the same time, playing some part in fostering 'horizontal' liaison and a common way of working within the cluster.

In this work it was crucial that the cascade teacher realized that his/her role was not to do with the provision of an extra pair of hands in the classroom but was concerned with the professional development of the teacher in the school with whom he/she was working. As with the full-time advisory teachers, their most important attribute was having the personality and ability to lead colleagues in the management of change. Secondly they needed to be familiar with the processes of science and design technology as well as having expertise over a wide age range. Clearly, in terms of management skills, as with the advisory teacher team, it was useful to recruit from those who had followed an appropriate management course. The final team, chosen on the grounds of personality in addition to expertise, had very varied backgrounds. The first term was spent in extending their experience and required individualized training, partly at the Centre and partly accompanying the advisory teachers into schools. Each cascade member had some ten to twelve days of direct support and familiarization before they worked on their own. Evidence provided by a questionnaire showed that although members of the cascade team initially felt apprehensive, a little worried and inadequate, the training had enabled them to ideas and gain confidence. Afterwards, most felt that they could offer their expertise to other schools and were eager to start work.

The advisory teacher for design technology and science, also newly appointed in 1986, was responsible for the day-to-day coordination and well being of the team. He regularly visits the schools in which they are working, provides additional training and support as required and, most importantly, takes on a pastoral role acting as a friend and counsellor. In particular, reassurances were necessary to overcome the early lack of confidence and feeling of isolation. In spite of this, however, it was obvious that the spectre of starting the job stayed with them until they had their first success with staff in school. The initial placement was thus crucial. To ensure success, the schools were hand picked as those needing help but which were not so resistant to change that cascade team members would not have time to grow into the job. As a result of their work in schools, problems did inevitably arise. To cope with these and also to allow for resourcing and, more importantly, to maintain a good team atmosphere, a limited number of 'in-days' were built into the programme. These were days when the cascade team would come into the centre to discuss common problems with their team leader and other members of the team. Currently, these days are being increasingly used for additional training requested by team members. The cascade teachers themselves valued this idea highly. It gave them the opportunity to work as a group, which they found to be extremely useful and stimulating, particularly because of the opportunity afforded for discussion, mutual support and the sharing of experiences. The situation described is perhaps a true example of what is meant by the term 'training the trainers'.

It was inevitable that adopting the approach of appointing ten part-time cascade personnel, there were a number of advantages and disadvantages to be considered. These are set out below.

Advantages

1. The provision of teachers with maximum credibility who increase the variety of experience within the ESG team.
2. The provision of career and professional development opportunities for a greater number of teachers.
3. The opportunity of management experience for the advisory teacher responsible for the day-to-day running of the cascade team.

4. The lower cost to the LEA.

5. An uncomplicated re-entry and after-care procedure.
6. The long-term benefits to the LEA are spread over a greater number of schools.

Disadvantages

1. The dual loyalty imposed on cascade team members.

2. The isolation felt by the teachers concerned.

3. The resource implications for the LEA.

4. The difficulty of securing appropriate supply cover.
5. The considerable increase in management time required.
6. The overall effectiveness compared with a full-time advisory teacher.

The greatest advantage was that the enhancement of the original ESG team was made possible. By the simple decision to employ ten teachers, the LEA could appoint individuals with a variety of experience and background not possible in two full-time advisory teachers. Thus, the team has included an Asian teacher with extensive multicultural experience, a special education teacher, and a number of teachers with experience of a variety of pupil age ranges who also had expertise in a particular subject area. This enriched the whole team in a very positive manner. Furthermore, an initial problem faced by all ESG full-time advisory teachers had been to establish and maintain credibility in the schools. This has not proved to be a difficulty where cascade teachers are working four days per week with their own classes.

The cascade teachers also benefited as individuals. The opportunities for most primary school teachers to visit other schools, let alone other classes in their own school, are sadly very limited. To work in a county team, to develop management and interpersonal skills by working as a cascade team teacher and take a positive part in curriculum development in more than one school, offer the individual a unique chance which has already proved to be of value in career development terms. The burden of the Authority to enable professional development for its employees is facilitated by the setting up of a cascade team whereby at least five times the number of teachers are having the above opportunities. In cost terms under this system these opportunities are relatively cheap, but nevertheless very effective in the general promotion of primary science and design technology.

Additionally, professional development opportunity was provided for the advisory teacher for design technology and science. Although the overall responsibility lay with the inspector, who acted as consultant, he was given a chance to develop his managerial skills in coordinating the cascade team, developing an ongoing training programme and in taking on a pastoral role. With regard to cost to the LEA, the formation of a 'cascade' team was advantageous. The deceptively simple equation of two full-time advisory teachers as equivalent to ten 'cascade' teachers (at one day per week) is misleading. The Bedfordshire cascade team was seconded on their existing salaries. In common with many other LEAs, Bedfordshire decided that it was necessary to allocate a sufficiently high salary to attract well qualified personnel as advisory teachers. In reality, ten part-time teachers represented a significantly lower cost to the Authority.

Another advantage to the Authority concerned the 'after-care' of team members. As the first phase of the ESG projects are coming to a close, many LEAs are facing a problem of re-entry of the advisory teachers into schools. Not all have secondment from their original schools, unlike the cascade team. Teachers returning to their school from a period as a member of a cascade team is relatively straightforward, resumption from four days per week to a full-time appointment being an uncomplicated step. In addition to the benefits to the individual and the LEA, it is confidently felt that there will be significant long term benefits to the providing school or cluster, given that proper use is made of the experiences gained by the teacher on resumption of his/her fulltime post.

There are, however, several serious disadvantages. As many LEAs have experienced, two part-time posts usually add up in terms of commitment to more than one full-time post. This inevitably puts a strain on the conscientious teacher. This point, made strongly by headteachers from other LEAs, is felt no less strongly in Bedfordshire. However committed, it is inevitable that there will be some effects on both positions held by the cascade teacher; the main one being that which is felt by the providing school as reported by the headteachers concerned. Heads usually compromise on this point, however, and look forward to the benefits which the cascade teacher will bring back to their school.

This stress must also be endured alongside the undoubted isolation felt by the cascade teacher. All the cascade team highly valued the rare opportunities to meet together for mutual support and exchange of experiences. These occasions must be balanced against the primary need to have the team working with colleagues in the schools. This balance has not been easy to achieve.

Initially, an additional difficulty, the solution of which had financial implications for the LEA, concerned the resourcing of the cascade team. For obvious reasons, cascade teachers were placed in schools near to their own, which may have been some distance from the Primary Science and Technology Centre. Since there was no time available for travel, it was necessary to resource each of the ten separately. Full time advisory teachers, by contrast, inevitably visit the Centre more frequently and can make use of central resources more economically.

Another crucial factor, was the provision of appropriate supply cover. The release of a teacher to join the cascade team involves replacement for one day per week by a supply teacher, with some considerable disruption, particularly for younger children. Many head-teachers experienced considerable difficulty in finding suitable supply teachers. In urban areas this problem is particularly difficult and has also been felt in other parts of the county.

By far the most serious disadvantage, however, was the increase in time required to manage a team of ten part-timers as opposed to two full-time personnel. As described above, the cascade team is managed on a day-to-day basis by the full-time advisory teacher for design technology and science and, in terms of pastoral support particularly, this may correspond to a five-fold increase in time required. Training days and general oversight of work also represent an additional time commitment. Each team member also works in conjunction with one of the other advisory teachers in a particular school cluster and needs support in this respect. The primary science and technology inspector is also heavily involved in the overall management of the team, particularly with regard to turnover in personnel. As already noted, cascade teachers have seen the career opportunities offered by the experience and have taken advantage of this. Of the original ten, four have moved on for various reasons, making the introduction of new teachers necessary, with considerable training implications. On the plus side, however, this does enable a larger number of teachers to have the cascade experience. All of this adds up to a considerable time commitment which cannot be used elsewhere and which must be added into the whole equation when the total effectiveness of the operation is being considered. Finally, it must be recognized that the overall effectiveness of the individual part-time cascade teacher is in no way equivalent to the full-time advisory teacher, due to the differences in the time available to each to gain experience and develop expertise.

On balance, the appointment of ten part-time cascade team teachers to work alongside an established full-time team and was the correct one in spite of the disadvantages. Most importantly, the appointments significantly enhanced the total expertise within the Centre team. Also, the experience provided a relatively large number of individuals professional development and career opportunities which they would perhaps otherwise not have gained. Furthermore, after the members of the cascade team returned to their schools, the possibilities of sharing the expertise gained, either within individual schools or within a local 'cluster' group, was an important factor in setting up the model initially. In terms of cost effectiveness, both in financial and time expenditure, the cascade model of development is one which needs very much careful thought before it is entered into. It is a model which is perhaps set up for the purpose of achieving certain short-term goals or perhaps initiated and used by an LEA as a strategy for its own development.

The monitoring of the cost effectiveness of a particular management structure within an LEA is inevitably a long term process. Adjustments are, therefore, of a long term nature, particularly since temporary appointments or secondments are involved. However, the experience and expertise gained in Bedfordshire is seen to be invaluable in terms of the implementation of the requirements of the National Curriculum over the next few years. It is hoped that the observations made are of some help to other LEAs considering similar courses of action.

Chapter 8

Some Thoughts on the Future

Introduction

From September 1989, Primary Schools have been expected to implement the requirements of the National Curriculum in the core subjects for a reasonable amount of time. Most LEAs in the country provided training for coordinators in the core subjects of English, mathematics and science during the summer term of 1989. Training in the core subjects for the whole school was facilitated through an extra school-closure day. Such training, because of the time awarded to it, can only be considered to be 'awareness raising' for headteachers and teachers. The implementation of real change, it has been recognized, will take much longer to achieve, as indicated in the earlier chapters. Some of the complex issues surrounding the changes necessary in the teaching of science and design technology to children aged between 3–13 have been raised in this book.

Perhaps now is the time to consider possibilities for the way ahead for those immediately concerned with the continued implementation of the National Curriculum. That is the LEA, individual headteachers, the classroom practitioner, the pupils and, last but not least, the parents and governors. What will their role be in the implementation of the necessary change and which factors will exert the most influence?

The Local Education Authority

There is no doubt that the requirements of the National Curriculum have already caused LEAs to review their mode of operation. The areas identified below will need to be given particular attention.

Management Style

Local Education Authorities which promote collaborative ways of working throughout the system are likely to be the ones which will exert the most influence. Team work is essential if the abilities of pupils are to be influenced and developed. This notion extends throughout the system, as already stated, provided that each member of the team knows how to contribute and play their part. Genuine communication needs to exist between members and officers of the LEA and those members and officers who support the LEA function from other departments. Similarly, the same kind of communication needs to exist between the LEA and each school. Each school with increased autonomy under the local management arrangements will need to ensure that good professional communication exists, supported by informed collaboration from the governors and parents. In many ways it is essential that the communication system is set up quickly as the promotion of learning cannot easily take place without it; if the quality of that learning is to be improved then the collaborative communication network described above will help to improve the quality of the provision as a whole.

Structure In Relation to Function

Because of the increasing need to not only provide the support required to implement the National Curriculum but also to monitor its delivery, it will be necessary to re-examine the roles of the personnel operating within the Authority and adjust the balance in relation to the function of the various components. For example, it may be necessary to increase the numbers of inspectors/advisers within an Authority in order that each may act in a supportive capacity as an adviser but also carry out an inspectoral role. Alternatively, it may be more appropriate to limit the monitoring and inspectoral role to inspectors and set up a tier of advisory teachers to provide the necessary support to schools and individual teachers.

The Monitoring Process

Information will need to be monitored carefully both by the school and by an 'independent' group of inspectors maintained nationally and locally for this purpose. The views of this group of people will need to be expressed independently of one another, yet it would be an advantage if the criteria for the formulation of such views were to be drawn up collaboratively by the two groups. Data collected from this form of curriculum monitoring will provide the evidence on which decisions about the future need for change can be based.

Advisory Support

The most effective way to influence curriculum change is in the classroom using advisory support to work alongside teachers who will be implementing the necessary changes. Once again there is a danger in withdrawing this kind of support too soon before the sustained change is in the mind and practice of the teacher(s) concerned. Some schools may be capable of providing their own school-based in-service support. It may just so happen that a number of teachers from the school, including the head, may have attended various forms of in-service training occasions; if the results of the products of all these occasions happen to come together in the right way, then the school becomes an example of a self improving school. Such schools are always aware, however, that there are support mechanisms available external to the school and will tend to exploit these to the fullest extent.

Resource Provision

It has been true for a long time that sufficient resources should be deployed to ensure the efficient maintenance of the system. An interesting calculation to carry out would be by what proportion might it be necessary to increase the resourcing of change, in order that the system can effectively be improved at the fastest possible rate.

Establishing a Centre for Primary Science and Design Technology

Improvements to experiential areas of the curriculum, such as science and design technology, will need resource support in the first instance. This is true of most schools, but small schools in particular will require considerable help. To implement the National Curriculum effectively will require certain items of equipment, such as measuring implements, to be available in the classroom at all times. Other items will be needed at particular points in time and the establishment of a central LEA resource will be crucial in providing this kind of support as part of a rolling programme. Alongside this is the need to help schools resource themselves; this can only be done over an extended time period if available funding is not to be diluted and thus rendered ineffective. The establishment of a centre to organize and monitor such support is a crucial ingredient in the implementation of the changes required by the National Curriculum.

In-service Training and Development

For the immediate future, a central provision for science and design technology will be necessary if the enormous changes in primary schools are to be seen through to a stage which is self-sustaining. If support is withdrawn too early then all the effort to date — including the resource input so far — will have largely been wasted. A justification for this statement runs like this: a large number of teachers are employed in primary schools, many of whom did not have the full benefit of a complete science education themselves. In itself this may not be a great disadvantage provided that sufficient funding is made available for their in-service training and development. The effect of the improved science and design technology content of initial training courses will not come through the system for some time. Even then, as argued in chapter 6, it will be necessary to provide second and third level training if the quality of the provision is to improve beyond a standard minimum.

Once the need for the provision of second and third level training has become established, it may be recognized that this more advanced in-service training and development may be common to many areas of the primary curriculum. The role of universities, institutes and colleges of higher education must be recognized as providers of this kind of training and development who, in turn, should recognize the development which has taken place at the local level and make efforts to provide for the new requirements to be made of them.

The Headteacher

Those existing qualities, found in the good headteacher, will need to be added to, developed and extended. Predictably the role of headteacher in the future will be more demanding and therefore without doubt, become the most important part of the system under the 1988 Education Reform Act.

Take one traditional quality to be found in headteachers; that of leadership. The selection process applied to headteachers will need to recognize the new qualities and pressures which headteachers will need to have and to endure in the role. Headteachers will still need to be the leading professional in the school and prove frequently that they are good teachers. At the same time throughout their development they will need to be systematically exposed to different levels of leadership and management training in order to fulfil the demands of the role. Those members of the LEA and the governing body involved with the selection process for the appointment of a new headteacher also have a more difficult and demanding task to perform. Once appointed, the leadership qualities of the individual will begin to have an effect.

In the context of this book, one aspect of a headteacher's role which appears to have been neglected under the 1988 Legislation is that of the responsibility of providing in-service training and development for staff. It is seen to be essential that all new heads appointed at least recognize they have responsibilities in this area of leadership. This is seen by the authors as a necessary additional requirement for all headteachers in the future. In addition to his/her leadership qualities in the more open management situation required for development he/she will need to continually consider the judgments made concerning the delegation of responsibility and authority. Judgments in this area, correctly and conscientiously applied, will allow other members of staff to grow and develop in their responses to children's needs. The qualities will need to be extended in two senses, one by recognizing the extended school community, parents, governors and friends of the school, second, by recognizing the needs and roles and providing for them. This will be most necessary as the ERA appears, initially, at any rate, to be more concerned with the administrative procedures associated with resource allocation. Though the concept of Local Management of Schools (LMS) does recognize the wider role and responsibility, much of which will be devolved to the headteacher, he/she, as a consequence, will need to be very strong in his/her resolve to ensure that the curriculum provided for the pupils is kept clearly in the central focus and not distracted by issues like LMS or Open Enrolment. The implementation of the National Curriculum must not come second best to those other provisions of the Act. It is therefore necessary, if the sentiments contained in the following quotation are to be fulfilled, to continue to provide the resources and encouragement to schools and LEA's to develop their potential for the benefit of all children.

> Despite the good performance of some schools, too many pupils are still achieving less than they could and less than they should, compared with children of other leading European countries. The overall picture is one of disappointingly low standards of achievement. Teachers' expectations of what their pupils can achieve are frequently low. Today's school curriculum can often be narrow and unbalanced. For example, too many boys give up Modern Languages before they are sixteen. Too many girls drop Physical Sciences. A National Curriculum will guarantee that all pupils receive an education which is broad, balanced, relevant to their needs and set in a clear moral framework. It will prepare them better for adult responsibilities and work at the same time by setting clear targets and monitoring progress, it aims to raise the standards achieved by pupils and schools. (DES, 1989b)

This statement clearly sets out an agenda for action, one with which most headteachers and teachers would agree in general terms. Elsewhere it has been stated that the implementation of the National Curriculum can only be achieved over a period of time. The implications of this admission are that the implementation of the National

Curriculum can only be achieved if the implementation of the core, foundation and other subjects are phased in over a period of time and that time, money and effort is applied to help the delivery. The responsibility of the headteacher to ensure that all children (and teachers) achieve the minimum standards laid down and those children capable of achievement beyond the minimum requirement have every opportunity to do so is tremendous.

Calls upon the leadership strengths of individual headteachers to provide and oversee in-service occasions will also be tremendous. Not all headteachers, however, can or will want to lead all in-service occasions. Responsibility in these cases can be delegated to members of staff, for example, curriculum coordinators or those working externally to the school who can provide the advisory support necessary. The good head will know the development which he/she can initiate, those which can be delegated within the school and those which are best left to be fulfilled by external advisory support.

Heads should not be left unsupported in making these important decisions. A team of LEA inspectors will be needed to monitor and help by making recommendations which will effect the heads' judgment about the support which is required. Resources for centrally-based and school-based in-service support will, to emphasize the point yet again, need to be provided until the desired development in the school is judged to be self-sustaining or permanent as the case may be. Headteachers have always argued that they play a most vital role, yet the requirements of the future make the role even more vital and more difficult to achieve holistically, if standards are to be raised for all children.

The Teacher

Headteachers lead and manage the school on a daily basis. Unless it is a very small school, the role of the class teacher and/or the curriculum coordinator is also vital. The class teacher will need confidence to deliver the National Curriculum (including the requirement to assess pupils in a different way), be open minded about the nature of the subject matter being delivered, trust colleagues who are responsible for the delivery of the proceeding stages, assess pupil performance as accurately as possible and above all, keep a sense of proportion and good humour about the developments taking place over the next ten years.

Most teachers have nothing to fear about the National Curriculum as the requirements, for the most part, are already in place or are being developed. The framework provided by the National Curriculum, against which judgments about the teaching and learning situation can be made, should be seized upon and developed into a professional tool to aid the development needed for the future.

The Pupils

Initially the pupils should not be able to recognize too much change except that their day in school becomes more varied and interesting as new activities and challenges are introduced. The continuous assessment requirement relevant to a particular area of the curriculum should keep the activity in perspective, but at the same time, it should not become a device which narrows and limits what is offered. Children of primary school age will still need opportunity to experiment with their own ideas in the safety of the confines of the teaching/learning situation. Their teachers will need to learn occasionally to observe their children performing the tasks which have been designed in order to add to their knowledge of an individual and the progress which he/she is making.

The preservation of the child's autonomy for the progressive acquisition and control of their own learning is a fundamental requirement of good educational practice. At the same time the children's own professional autonomy has to be preserved in the complexities which exist in a good classroom. To provide an experience which is, 'broad, balanced and relevant to their needs and set in a clear moral framework', is difficult enough, but the breadth, balance and relevance must also provide for the progressive development and acquisition of the 'basic' skills, concepts, knowledge, attitudes and values of all pupils in at least a dozen subject areas.

Over a considerable number of years the best primary practice has shown how the delicate balance required between the pupils' learning and the teachers' teaching can be managed to good effect and for the benefit of the children. The key stage testing of children at the ages of 7, 11, 14 and 16 should at least allow this aspect of primary practice to be extended to the age of 16 and beyond. If sufficiently targeted resources can continue to be made available to allow the curricular provision to be well managed and organized, there is no doubt the children of today will be the guardians of a secure scientific and technological future.

Parents and Governors

Without parents there would be no need for schools, maintained or non-maintained. They have, as the ERA sets out, a right to know about their own child's progress. This simple single fact in the initial stages of the implementation process could well be the subject of some difficulty in communication and misunderstanding between the partners associated with the child's development. Generally speaking, the professionals have not been good at developing the communication skills necessary to allow parents to obtain a real indication of their own child's developing ability. Sometimes parents are too 'expert' about their perceptions and expectations of an educational system which has developed, and is developing, since their own schools days. Parents are looking for and governors have the responsibility of providing for improvements in opportunity, therefore, the quality of the change process must be good and explained to parents, so that they can judge the effect of those changes on their own child for themselves. Once again, time and effort will need to be devoted by the partners in the system if the communication of understanding of the developing abilities of the child are to be clearly articulated.

The provision under the Act for parents to become governors of schools, with increased responsibilities, will also need some care and attention in the early stages. Help in the form of training will be and is being provided.

Conclusion

The four corners of the partnership in schools, the pupils, the staff, the parents and governors, supported, monitored, evaluated and advised by the centrally based staff and policies of the LEA in its new role, is the scenario of the future. Whilst schools are undergoing such radical changes it is essential that all partners are kept informed of the attempted changes and continue to support the efforts of the professionals involved.

Finally, curricular experiences in science and design technology are more likely to develop if the school recognizes that is has the ability to improve itself. Once the 'scenario of the future' is recognized fully by the school community, it, in turn, is more likely to be supportive of the efforts made, rather than adopting a critical stance which ultimately becomes destructive. However, the professional development for a school which is embarking on the road of self improvement cannot take place in a vacuum; the realities of the situation prevailing at any one time must be taken into consideration. This book attempts to analyze the factors which need to be taken into account by a school which intends to progress along this route. The workshops in Part 2 provide a means to help such a school progress.

References

ALEXANDER, D. and PENNELL, A. (1981) 'A Model for the Implementation of Primary Science; *British Journal of In-Service Education*, vol 7, no. 3.

BAINBRIDGE, J. W., STOCKDALE, R. W. and WASTNEDGE, E. R. (1967/1970) *Teachers' Guide 1 and 2*. The Nuffield Junior Science Project. London, Glasgow: Collins.

BEDFORDSHIRE EDUCATION SERVICE (1988) *Early Explorations*. Ampthill: Teaching Media Resource Service.

BEDFORDSHIRE EDUCATION SERVICE (1988) *Playing with Natural Materials*. Ampthill: Teaching Media Resource Service.

BEDFORDSHIRE EDUCATION SERVICE (1989) *National Curriculum Training Manual For Schools, The Core, Key Stage 1: Programmes of Study*. Ampthill: Teaching Media Resource Service.

BEDFORDSHIRE EDUCATION SERVICE (1989) *National Curriculum Training Manual For Schools, The Core, Key Stage 1: Assessment and Reading*. Ampthill: Teaching Media Resource Service.

BEDFORDSHIRE EDUCATION SERVICE (1989) *National Curriculum Training Manual for Schools Design and Technology, Key Stages 1 and 2: Programmes of Study*. Ampthill: Teaching Media Resource Service.

BRITISH SCIENCE AND TECHNOLOGY IN EDUCATION (1988) *Solving Problems with Electronics*. Carlton: British Science and Technology in Education (BSTE).

Design and Technology for Ages 5–16. (DES) (1989) London: HMSO.

FULLAN, M. (1986) 'The Management of Change' in HOYLE and MCMAHON, A. (eds.), *The Management of Schools*, London: Kogan Page.

HARLEN, W., DARWIN, A. and MURPHY, M. (1978) *Match and Mismatch*. Edinburgh: Oliver and Boyd.

HOLLY, P. and SOUTHWORTH, G. (1989) *The Developing School*, Lewes, Falmer Press.

HOPKINS, D. (1987) 'Implications for School improvement at local level' in HOPKINS, D. (ed.) *Improving the Quality of Schooling*. Lewes: Falmer Press.

LIPPITT, R., WATSON, J. and WESTLEY, B. (1958) *The Dynamics of Planned Change*. New York: Harcourt, Brace & Co.

National Curriculum: From Policy to Practice. DES (1989). London: HMSO.

PENNELL, A., PETRIE, P. and BENT, G. (1989) 'Making the Most of ESG Funding', *British Journal of In-service Education*, vol 15, no 2.

Primary Education in England (1978). A survey by HM Inspectors of Schools. London: HMSO.

SCHOOLS COUNCIL, (1978) *Learning through Science*. Formulating a School Policy. London and Milwaukee: Macdonald Education.

SCHOOLS COUNCIL, (1972) *Science 5–13*. With Objectives in Mind. London and Milwaukee: Macdonald Educational.

Science in the National Curriculum. DES (1989). London: HMSO.

STENHOUSE, L., (1975) *An Introduction to Curriculum Research and Development*. London: Heinemann.

THE OPEN UNIVERSITY. (1980) *Curriculum in Action*. An Approach to Evaluation. Milton Keynes: The Open University Press.

PART 2
Change Tactics

Introduction

Chapter 5, 'Implementing a policy for change within a school', introduces the use of a framework for bringing about the desired change. In the framework, a number of discussion phases are interspersed with appropriate action phases and progress between the two is achieved by the application of a series of tactics. Those which are designed to facilitate discussion are referred to as Discussion Tactics while those which bring about a course of action are called Action Tactics. This general idea is then developed and applied specifically to the implementation of the National Curriculum in Chapter 6. An important point to make here is that each tactic is designed to bring about a course of action in specific circumstances, and that different tactics might well be used to bring about the same course of action.

What follows, in this part of the book, is a series of Discussion and Action Tactics which can be modified and adapted for use in school. Once teachers have gained in confidence, they will want to design their own tactics to help them implement the National Curriculum or, indeed, to bring about any other form of change within the school. Each tactic is presented in the form of a workshop which may focus upon a practical exercise, a brainstorming session, a quiz, a role play activity and so on. It is intended that some of the workshops can be used on their own whilst others form part of a series.

Contents

Each workshop has a schedule for participants and a course leader's guide. The latter seeks to provide a rationale for the workshop, guidance on its introduction in the form of a paraphrase, a resume of points which might or should be raised in discussion and details of the time required for each section.

These are outlined below and refer to specific parts of the development framework outlined in Chapter 6.

Discussion Tactics 1

Accountability
Why science and design technology should be included in the basic curriculum	Role play exercise

Planning the Development
Identifying needs — *What* needs to be done?	Questionnaire school self analysis
Responding to *Needs* — *How* can we do it?	Brainstorming exercise
Formulating the programme — *When* would it be appropriate?	Forward planning exercise

Coordination
The role of the curriculum coordinator	Brainstorming exercise

Action Tactics 1

Understanding the Science and Design Technology 'Process'
What do we mean by science and design technology education?	True/false workshop

Working Objectively
Why teach science and design technology?	Brainstorming exercise
Planning a topic objectively	Forward planning exercise

Implementing Programmes of Study
Development of a theme	'Hands On' workshop
Familiarization with Attainment Targets	Practical workshop

Finding out about Resources
The school site — maximizing the potential of the school environment	Planning exercise
Curriculum Development Projects — An evaluation	Group evaluation

Being Familiar with Safety Matters
Safety quiz	Quiz
Safety matters	Practical workshop

Discussion Tactics 2

Formulating a School Policy
Policy versus syllabus   Use of a nominal group technique

Action Tactics 2

Assessing Childrens' Science and Design Technology Level
    Introducing a criterion-referenced   Practical activities
    check list
    Using a criterion-referenced check list   Practical activities
    Assessing children's science and   Discussion based upon 'trigger' material.
    design technology level   (slide/tape and video)
    Designing and assessing activities   Theoretical workshop

Matching, Continuity and Progression
    The progressive development of   Evaluation of classroom implementation
    investigative skills
    The progressive development of   Theoretical workshop
    concepts
    Identifying a conceptual progression   Discussion based upon children's work
    'Matching'   Forward planning exercise
    Planning a differentiated topic   Theoretical workshop

Curriculum Balance
    Curriculum analysis   Use of case study material
    Curriculum review   Analytical exercise

Using the Workshops in School

Each workshop requires about one to one and a half hours of time to complete and thus each can be used as a unit for school focused INSET. Whilst some workshops stand alone, others form part of a series of two or more. Some are particularly suited for use at the end of a working day since they require time either for consolidation or research before embarking upon the next one in the series. Others are best used in a block providing an excellent focus for a training day, or a series of after school meetings.

Workshops particularly suitable for INSET after school

1.   Workshops which can be used in isolation:
        The role of the curriculum coordinator
        Why science and design technology should be included in the basic curriculum
        Policy versus syllabus
        Safety quiz
        Safety matters

2.   Workshops which need to be spaced out in time for research and/or consolidation:
        Identifying needs — *What* needs to be done?
        Responding to needs — *How* can we do it?
        Formulating the programme — *When* would it be appropriate?
3.   Workshops which rely on previous research:
        The school site — maximizing the potential of the school environment
        Curriculum development projects — an evaluation
        Curriculum analysis
        (Note that this workshop forms part of a series.)

Workshops particularly suitable for use as a block on training days

Block 1
        What do we mean by Science and Design Technology Education?
        Why teach Science and Design Technology?
        Planning a topic objectively
        Development of a theme
        Familiarization with Attainment Targets

Block 2
        Introducing a criterion — referenced check list
        Using a criterion — referenced check list
        Assessing children's Science and Design Technology level
        Designing and assessing activities

Block 3
        The progressive development of investigative skills
        The progressive development of concepts
        Identifying a conceptual progression
        'Matching'
        Planning a differentiated topic

Block 4
        Curriculum Analysis
        Curriculum Review
        Record Keeping

Discussion Tactics 1

Discussion Tactics 1: Accountability

Workshop 1: Why Science and Design Technology Should Be Included in the Basic Curriculum

Leader's Guide

You may believe that science and design technology are both relevant and important to children of 5–16 years. However, in trying to understand their introduction into the basic curriculum of your school, colleagues and others may need reassurance and seek clarification.

Some of the main issues you may have to face are:

1. We don't know what primary science and design technology are all about.
2. We don't have any scientific or technological knowledge, so how can we teach them?
3. There's no time to do it.
4. There aren't enough resources available.

This workshop is designed not only to enable yourself and colleagues to anticipate and discuss some of these arguments in advance, but also to invite staff to consider the way ahead in their own school.

Introduction — 10 minutes — whole group

Put over the points made in the box below:

> Now we have to include science and design technology in the school curriculum we need, as a staff to be able to explain their inclusion in case we are ever put in a position where this is necessary. What I am talking about is accountability; we need to be accountable to all kinds of people, school governors, parents and so on. Because of this, it might be a good idea to clarify our thinking by means of an 'in house' exercise.

Introduce the workshop as a means of coming to terms with the problem of arriving at a consensus view but also stress its use in terms of rehearsing real situations beforehand.

Implementation

1.1 Workshop — 5 minutes — in pairs

Ask colleagues to work in pairs and choose one of the roles indicated on the sheet. You will undoubtedly get opposition from a few who object to taking on a role they would not play in real life; you will need to try to persuade them to 'have a go' for the sake of the others and arrange an opportunity to exchange roles if necessary.

If colleagues are unaccustomed to role play techniques *stress the need to 'act' and enter into the exercise with some degree of seriousness*! It may help if they imagine a situation where a governor or headteacher (role 2) is talking to a parent or worried teacher (role 1).

1.2 — 10 minutes — individually

Now ask colleagues, *individually*, to write down as many arguments as possible to support their case.

It is important at this stage that the arguments are *written down* and that no discussion is allowed.

1.3 — 15 to 20 minutes — in pairs

When everyone is ready, ask them to decide on a particular context or situation and begin to argue.

2. Discussion — 30 minutes — whole group

   Ask each pair, in turn, for a contribution. A number of issues will be raised but the focus should be on arguments for and against the inclusion of science and design technology within the curriculum of the school.

3. Conclusion — 15 minutes — whole group

   As a group, compile a list of arguments for and against the above issue.

It is interesting that, during the trial of this particular workshop, teachers who were initially disinterested commented, retrospectively, in very favourable terms after having had to 'play it for real' in school!

Accountability

Workshop 1: Why Science and Design Technology Should Be Included in the Curriculum

This workshop is designed not only to enable you to anticipate and discuss in advance arguments for the inclusion of science and design technology within the basic curriculum, but also to consider the way ahead in your own school.

1. Workshop
   1.1 Work in pairs and choose one role each:
   Role 1. You feel that:
   The curriculum is too crowded. There isn't time to do science and design technology properly and still give time to the basics.
   Role 2. You feel that:
   Schools must now take on the responsibility for the scientific and technological aspects of education.
   1.2 Write down arguments you could use to support your case.
   1.3 When told to do so, argue your case.
2. Open-forum discussion: 'Why science and design technology should be included in the basic curriculum'.
3. Conclusion
   Compile a list of arguments for and against the above issue in the space below.

Discussion Tactics 1: Planning the Development

Workshop 1.1: Identifying Needs — *What* needs to be done?

Leader's Guide

A crucial factor to be taken into consideration in planning a development programme is the attitude of colleagues to the curriculum area in question.

1. Administration of the questionnaire
    Before embarking on the programme, the administration of a questionnaire to all the teachers involved has been found to be a useful preparatory step. You are asked, therefore, prior to any curriculum development meeting, to ask all colleagues to complete the attached check list and return the completed forms to you for analysis. *Stress that it is anonymous.*
2. Analysis of questionnaires
    Hopefully you will have with you the check lists completed by colleagues. If you have not already done so, enter all scores on the spare sheet provided to give you an overview of the staff of your school. Now list all those issues identified on the bottom part of the questionnaire, if necessary, grouping them in some way.

    You will now be in a position to make a list of the stated difficulties/needs of your colleagues in priority order. Does this list match the problems *you* know to exist?
3. Evaluation of the exercise
    Do you think your colleagues answered truthfully or did their replies reflect the views they thought you would like them to express? Whatever happened in your case, the objective of actually raising the issues will have been achieved and you colleagues will be more aware of the factors involved.

Science and Design Technology Questionnaire

So we can see how well equipped we are, as a school, to implement the National Curriculum in science and design/technology in all classes, I am asking staff to fill in the questionnaire below. This may be carried out anonymously if you wish but I would be grateful if forms could either be left in the box provided in the staff room or returned to me.

How would you rate yourself with regard to teaching science and design technology in school?

Please check the appropriate space on each scale.

I support the notion that science and design technology have a lot in common					I think that science and design technology are quite distinct

I teach little or no science or design technology, either as separate subjects or integrated with topic work					I teach a considerable amount of science and design technology to my children

I have considerable difficulty in understanding the sequences involved in the process of problem solving relevant to science and design technology					I have no difficulty whatsoever in understanding the process of problem solving in relation to science and design technology

I find that the process of identifying a range of appropriate problem solving activities for children is easy					I have great difficulty in identifying a range of appropriate activities for children i.e. getting ideas together
I find that I can organize science and design technology activities successfully					Organizing the work is very difficult

I find that the resources I need just are not available in school					The school is very well equipped — I can find all I need

Collecting the various bits and pieces needed takes very little effort					One of my main problems is in the collection of the various bits and pieces needed

I feel threatened by the thought of teaching science and design technology					I look forward to teaching science and design technology

I have no difficulty in planning a broad, balanced programme of practical science and design technology					I would not know where to begin in planning a programme of practical science and design technology

Please identify below those issues which you feel it would be useful to discuss as a group

....

....

....

Discussion Tactics 1: Planning the Development

Workshop 1.2: Identifying Needs — *What* needs to be done?

Leader's Guide

Experience has shown that, for many teachers, the thought of having to teach science and design technology is extremely threatening. The sooner it becomes apparent to them that others, perhaps even colleagues, feel the same way, the more rapidly progress is made.

This workshop enables teachers to share their individual difficulties and encourages them to begin to take a 'whole staff' approach to the problem.

Introduction — 5 minutes — whole group

Put over the points made in the box below:

> Although some of you have been providing scientific and technological activities for the youngsters in your classes for some time, others have been 'putting things off' for a number of reasons. Before we can begin to plan the way ahead, we really need to be able to identify, as a staff, the difficulties we face at present; having done that, it may be possible to take steps, at least, to alleviate some of them.

Implementation — 60 to 65 minutes (75 to 85 minutes for a large staff)

1. Workshop
    1.1 Identifying some common difficulties — 15 minutes — Individually
         Ask colleagues, individually, to list all the aspects of teaching science and design technology which they find difficult.
         It is important, at this stage, that you do not allow any discussion to take place since this only serves to act as a distractor.

    1.2 Identifying categories of difficulty — 30 minutes — small group or whole staff
         Ask group members to combine their individual lists and then sort the difficulties into categories.
         Since overlapping can occur this exercise may well take some time; it is important, however, that you allow colleagues enough time to consider each item fully. Examples of categories might be:
         Organization; Money; Starting Points; Policy; etc.
2. Discussion — 15 to 20 minutes — whole group (redundant if staff is small)
    Ask each group member to report on their findings.
3. Conclusion — 15 to 20 minutes — whole group
    Ask colleagues to compile an agreed list of categories and difficulties which apply to their school.
    Make it clear that this information will be used to help solve some of their problems in the next workshop.

Planning the Development

Workshop 1.2: Identifying Needs — *What* needs to be done?

Before we can decide on what needs to be done to help us include science and design technology in the curriculum of every class, we need to be able to identify some of the problems we face, as a staff, at present.

1. Workshop
   1.1 Identifying some common difficulties
       Individually, list all those aspects of science and design technology teaching which you find difficult.
   1.2 Identifying categories of difficulty
       Now, as a small group, combine lists and sort into categories.
2. Discussion
   Share the views of your group with the others involved.
3. Conclusion
   Compile an agreed list of categories and difficulties which apply to your school in the manner suggested below:

CATEGORY	DIFFICULTY
Starting points	Coping with an unidentified object brought into school on the spur of the moment
	Knowing what the scientific and technological aspects of a topic are
Organizing the children	

Discussion Tactics 1: Planning the Development

Workshop 2: Responding to Needs — *How* can we do it?

Leader's Guide

The idea that 'a problem shared is a problem halved' underlies the thinking behind this workshop which should follow the previous one within a short space of time. *Prior to the session, remind colleagues that they will all need the list compiled previously.*

Introduction — 5 minutes — whole group

Put over the points made in the box below:

Last time we compiled a joint list of difficulties which we felt were relevant to our particular school situation — you have brought the list along I hope! Today, I thought that we might 'have a go' at trying to solve some of the problems we identified although I accept that one or two, for example the ones involving finance, might have to be shelved until April.

Implementation — 45–70 minutes — small group or whole staff if small

1. Workshop — Overcoming difficulties – 35 minutes — small group
   Invite colleagues to consider each difficulty in turn and, as a small group, to make one or more suggestions for each, which might be of help in alleviating problem. Some suggestions are attached; also, *see the rest of this guide*. It is important that staff are encouraged, for the most part, to find solutions within their own school, but this should not imply that help gained from outside the institution is unimportant.
2. Discussion — 30 minutes — whole group (redundant if staff is small)
   Ask each group to report on each difficulty in turn, (remember that each group will be working on the same list). *At this stage it is important that you ask someone to record all the helpful suggestions made.*
3. Conclusion — 10 minutes — whole group
   Compile a composite list of helpful suggestions. *At this point, or before, you will need to introduce the ideas for workshops in this guide, so that they may be included in the list of possibilities.*

Planning the Development

Workshop 2: Responding to Needs — *How* can we do it?

Having identified both our individual and common problems in the last session, we are now in a position to move towards solving, at least, some of those problems as a whole staff.

1. Workshop — Overcoming difficulties
    Still working as a small group using the lists compiled before, consider ways in which each difficulty might be overcome.
    Record in tabular form as shown below:

CATEGORY	DIFFICULTY	HELPFUL SUGGESTION
Starting points	Coping with an unidentified object brought into school on the spur of the moment	Have magnifying equipment always available for observational work Keep a good selection of reference books in your classroom
	Knowing what the scientific and technological aspects of a topic are	Use 'Science in a Topic Topic' (Doug Kincaid) to help you
Organizing the children		

2. Discussion — Overcoming difficulties
3. Conclusion
    Compile a composite list of helpful suggestions on the attached sheet.

Responding To Needs — *How* can we do it?

CATEGORY	DIFFICULTY	HELPFUL SUGGESTION

Discussion Tactics 1: Planning the Development

Workshop 3: Formulating the Programme — *When* would it be appropriate?

Leader's Guide

The particular thinking behind this workshop is that the implementation of a curriculum development programme is much more likely to occur if all staff, including the head, are involved in its conception and planning. *Prior to the session remind colleagues that they will need the completed list of difficulties and helpful suggestions compiled previously.*

Introduction — 5 minutes — whole group

Put over the points made in the box below:

We have now reached a stage when we can begin to plan ahead! Everyone should have the list of problems and helpful ideas in front of them and, of course, it has already been established that the curriculum development focus for this academic year is going to be science and design technology.

However, we still need to be realistic in our planning and accept that, in order to achieve a substantial change, we are talking about a period of four or more years. We must not be tempted to do everything all at once but must, on the other hand, be vigilant in maintaining a steady momentum.

Implementation — 75 to 90 minutes

1. Workshop
    1.1 Identifying priorities — 15 minutes — small groups or whole staff if small
        Using the list of felt needs and suggestions for responding to those needs, identified as a result of the previous two workshops, ask colleagues to re-organize the list in priority order.
    1.2 Formulating a programme — 30 minutes — small group or whole staff if small
        Now ask them to devise a flow chart, with an appropriate time scale, to indicate the kind of school-based, whole and individual, staff activities which would be useful in bringing about the desired change. Warn them to consider the constraints which may be operating in the school at any one particular time, e.g. Christmas activities, parents' evenings, governors' meetings, etc.
2. Discussion — 15 minutes — whole group (redundant if staff is small)
    Ask each group to report in turn.
3. Conclusion — 25+ minutes — whole group
    Compile an agreed curriculum development programme.

Planning the Development

Workshop 3: Formulating the Programme — *When* would it be appropriate?

Having identified a number of common needs and given some thought to ways in which difficulties might be overcome, you are now in a position to consider the way ahead.

1. Workshop
   1.1 Identifying priorities
       As a small group, consider the list of difficulties (needs) in front of you and re-arrange them in priority order for your school.
   1.2 Formulating a programme

Working as a small group devise a flow chart (with a time scale) to indicate how curriculum development might proceed in school. You will need to consider constraints which may be operating in the system (school) and take these into account when designing your programme.

Record in tabular form as shown below:

TIME SCALE	FLOW CHART	CONSTRAINTS TAKEN INTO ACCOUNT
Autumn Term 3rd week	Inaugural meeting to discuss possibilities with colleagues	Organizational pressures at the start of a new year will have begun to ease — still enough time left in the term to make a positive start
Week preceeding half term	Workshops with colleagues on?	Sets the scene for the work to be initiated after half term
First four weeks after half term	Follow-up of workshop in the classroom situation	Duration short enough to be non-threatening — finishes before Christmas activities

2. Discussion
   Share the views of your group with the others involved.
3. Conclusion
   Compile an agreed flow chart using the attached sheet.

Formulating the Programme — *When* would it be appropriate?

TIME SCALE	FLOW CHART	CONSTRAINTS TAKEN INTO ACCOUNT

Discussion Tactics 1: Coordination

The Role of the Curriculum Coordinator

Leader's Guide

This workshop allows you to explore the various aspects of the curriculum coordinator's role and to share ideas.

Traditionally, in primary schools, subject definition has not been emphasized. However, with the introduction of the National Curriculum, presented as it is in terms of subject areas, it is even more important that the integration of the core curricular areas and others into thematic work is achieved. This implies that curriculum coordinators should not only be aware of their own particular role within the school, but also should strive to work with colleagues in the adoption of a cross curricular approach.

Another important observation to make is that the role is managerial in nature and thus most aspects of it will be common whatever the subject area. It is these common attributes with which this workshop is particularly concerned.

Introduction — 5 minutes — Whole group

Put over the points made in the box below:

> Well now, those of you with a curriculum responsibility must have a good idea of what your own particular job is about! Has it occurred to you, though, that some aspects of the role might be common to everyone whilst some aspects might be different? Also, do you envisage yourself operating individually or alongside others? How do you expect to relate to your headteacher and to colleagues? This workshop will allow us to explore all of these issues as well as identifying others which are of common concern.

Implementation — 50 Minutes — Mainly in about 3 small groups of 5 people

1. Brainstorming — 5 minutes — individually
    No discussion should be allowed during the exercise and people should be encouraged to compile a list as quickly as possible.
2. Discussion — 20 Minutes — small groups
    Use the attached table to record your findings before transfer to OHT. You will find that it will be easier if the group agrees the broad task categories first before fitting in the individual features and prioritizing.

    As you move round the groups try to introduce ideas which may not have been thought of. For example it is likely that the first category will be concerned with resources but will they have identified the professional development of colleagues as being important? Are they prepared to organize and lead school-based INSET or liaise with others such as the head, colleagues, parents and others?
3. Presentation — 15 Minutes — Whole group
    The most difficult aspect of managing this session, will be in keeping a tight control on the time element. Don't let the first group go on for too long. A useful phrase to use is 'I'm going to have to stop you in precisely one minute' and then do just that! For the groups, which follow on, you can ask them to only report on those categories and aspects of the role which are different.

4. Compilation of group findings — 10 Minutes — small groups
    The OHP transparencies should be passed round each of the groups in turn so that adjustments can be made. If you find that, at this stage, you are running out of time the findings can always be reproduced centrally and distributed later. However, it is obvious that it is best to avoid this chore if possible!

Plenary — 5 Minutes — Whole group

Now is the time to make the point that each participant has an outline job description for a curriculum coordinator. This can now be used as a basis for further discussion in school. Working in this way will ensure that the expectations of all concerned (the head, the Governors, the staff and the coordinator) have been taken into account thus preventing a gross mismatch.

Coordination

The Role of the Curriculum Coordinator

Work mainly in small groups.

1. Brainstorming:
   Work individually to identify the various features of the role and list these tasks.
2. Discussion:
   Now come together in your small group and share individual thinking. Make a combined list of features and divide this into task categories giving some indication of the importance of each group according to a 5 point scale. Transfer your findings on to OHP transparency.
3. Presentation:
   Each group should present their ideas in turn.
4. Compilation of group findings:
   Add any new ideas to your own list and re-prioritise your categories if necessary. You have now produced a job description for a curriculum co-ordinator which can be used as a basis for further discussion in school.

CATEGORY	FEATURE	IMPORTANCE LOW ↔ HIGH				
		1	2	3	4	5

Action Tactics 1

Action Tactics 1: Understanding the Science and Design Technology Process

Workshop 1: What Do We Mean by Science and Design Technology Education?

You may believe that science and design technology are both relevant and important to children of 5–13 years. However, in trying to introduce them into the curriculum of your school, colleagues and others may argue against it.

Some of the main issues you may have to face are:

1. We don't know what primary science and design technology is all about.
2. We don't have any scientific or technological knowledge, so how can we teach them?
3. There's no time to do them.
4. There aren't enough resources available.

This workshop is designed in anticipation of the first argument and will enable you to focus discussion not only on those issues which are relevant to science and design technology but also on those which are particularly important to colleagues.

1. Introduction — 5 minutes — whole group

   Put over the points made in the box below:

> Before we can make a start in school, we need to consider what *we* mean by science and design technology education. This is important because, unless all of use are saying the same thing, it will be impossible for us to achieve any continuity as children progress through the school and the pupils will be muddled in their responses.

Introduce the workshop as a light introduction which will allow colleagues to explore the issues you have just outlined in a relaxed manner. *Stress the fact that no 'fence sitting' is allowed.*

Implementation — 40+ minutes

1. Workshop — 10 minutes — in pairs
   Allow people to differ if agreement cannot be reached between each pair of participants.
2. Discussion — 30+ minutes — whole group
   Ask for a show of hands when exploring each statement in turn. Hopefully you will obtain agreement on a number of the statements, but those which have been 'loaded' *will allow you to discuss matters of balance* with colleagues. For example, in statement 5, some teachers will undoubtedly answer 'true', and this may well be so if a historical approach is taken (Pasteur's experiments), but since science should really be about children investigating at first hand, you will probably find that the majority of colleagues tick the 'false' column.
3. Conclusion — 15 minutes — whole group
   Try to come to a consensus about what science and design technology education *in your school* is concerned with.

   It is important here to let colleagues start from *where they are* but be prepared to work at modifying the statement later if it turns out to be less than appropriate.

Understanding the Science and Design Technology Process

Workshop 1: What Do We Mean by Science and Design Technology Education?

Before we can make a start in school, we need to consider what *we* mean by science and design technology education. The following workshop allows you to explore this issue.

1. In pairs discuss each statement and tick whether you consider it to be true or false.

TRUE   FALSE

1. Science and Design Technology is concerned with first-hand practical experience   _____ _____
2. Science and Design Technology is concerned with preparing children for life   _____ _____
3. Science and Design Technology is concerned with developing basic concepts   _____ _____
4. Science and Design Technology is concerned with language development   _____ _____
5. Science and Design Technology education is telling children about experiments   _____ _____
6. Science and Design Technology is about acquiring knowledge and skills   _____ _____
7. Science and Design Technology is concerned with appreciating patterns and relationships   _____ _____
8. Design Technology education is about making things properly   _____ _____
9. Science is concerned with reading about plants and animals   _____ _____
10. Design Technology is concerned with making something according to a brief   _____ _____
11. Science is concerned with writing up experiments correctly   _____ _____
12. Design Technology involves teaching children basic techniques   _____ _____
13. Science and Design Technology is about helping children interpret findings critically   _____ _____
14. Technology is about knowledge of materials   _____ _____
15. Science and Design Technology is concerned with developing aesthetic awareness   _____ _____
16. Science and Design Technology is concerned with showing children how things work   _____ _____
17. Science and Design Technology education is about developing children's observational skills   _____ _____
18. Science and Design Technology is concerned with passing on scientific techniques   _____ _____

19. Science and Design Technology is about communicating
    with others   _____ _____
20. Science and Design Technology education is concerned
    with getting across the right scientfic facts   _____ _____
21. Science and Design Technology is concerned with develop-
    ing children's curiosity   _____ _____
22. Science and Design Technology is mainly about electronics _____ _____
23. Science and Design Technology is concerned with testing
    and evaluating   _____ _____
24. Science education is about finding the right answer   _____ _____

2. Small group discussion.
3. Now write your views in the space below indicating the progression you would expect
   to see within your school.

   Science and Design Technology education is concerned with:

4. Open forum discussion.

Action Tactics 1: Working Objectively

Workshop 1: Why Teach Science and Design Technology?

Leader's Guide

Traditionally the majority of primary teachers plan their work with children from an
activity-based approach which does not necessarily take into account the particular needs of
individuals. Although they are quite clear about the various avenues to be explored in their
teaching, they do not relate these to any clearly defined objectives with the result that
'matching' does not always take place.

This activity allows teachers to clarify their ideas and sets the scene for the
implementation of an objective-based curriculum, an idea which is explored in the next
workshop.

Introduction — 10 minutes — whole group

Put over the points made in the box below:

> If we are to respond effectively to the National Curriculum Statutory Orders then we must be quite clear about *why* we are providing activities of a scientific and design technological nature for the children in our school. What is their purpose? What are *our* aims? How can we make them relevant to individual children?

You will need to introduce the idea of objectives which relate to the changes we expect to see in children as a result of the activities we provide for them, i.e. 'behavioural' objectives.

Implementation — 50 minutes

1. Workshop
   1.1 'Brainstorming' exercise — 20 minutes — in small groups
       During this activity you will be able to tell whether the term 'objective' needs further clarification. Remedy deficiencies as necessary with individuals.
   1.2 Classification of objectives — 15 minutes — in small groups
       Try to ensure, through discussion with each group, that the main categories chosen relate to the points you wish to raise in the discussion.
2. Discussion — 15 minutes — whole group
   As far as possible try to relate comments to the four main categories on the OHP transparency entitled 'WHY?' Use this as a concluding statement, pointing out that objectives on the left side of the diagram relate to the wider curriculum whilst, by and large, those on the right side relate more closely to the subject area in question, in this instance, science and design technology.

Working Objectively

Workshop 1: Why Teach Science and Design Technology?

If, as teachers, we are to provide a curriculum that is appropriate for all the children in our school, taking into account their individual differences, then one must assume that it needs to be created within a framework which is objective based.

1. Workshop
    1.1 Work in small groups and 'brainstorm' to produce a list of objectives for science and design technology education.
    1.2 Now sort your objectives into broad categories agreed within your group.
2. Discussion
    Finally, come together as a larger group and share views of objectives for science and design technology education with colleagues.

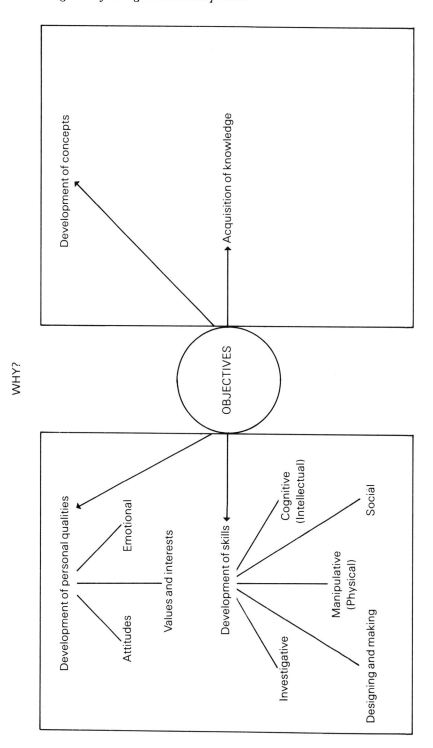

WHY?

Classification of Educational Objectives

Action Tactics 1: Working Objectively

Workshop 2: Planning a Topic Objectively

Leader's Guide

This workshop follows on from 'Why teach Science and Design Technology?', a workshop which seeks to help teachers clarify their ideas about objectives for science and design technology education.

In order to respond effectively to the National Curriculum, schools will need to move from an activity-based planning approach to one which seeks to implement a number of objective statements which have either been agreed informally or overtly incorporated in a school policy document.

This workshop is designed to help teachers come to terms with such an approach.

Introduction — 10 minutes — whole group

Put over the points made in the box below:

> Last time we managed to put together a number of objectives for science and design technology which we categorized under four broad headings. What I would like you to do now is to give some thought to the kind of activities you might use with children in order to achieve them. In other words, I am asking you to start your planning from the *objective* rather than the *activity*. In this way we stand a better chance of providing work which is appropriate to particular children, as well as allowing for balance continuity and progression within the curriculum.

Introduce the hand out concerned with objective statements, explaining that they have been collected from a number of published, objective-based curriculum development projects (do not let on that some are not science or design technology based) and arranged in four Piagetian development levels, according to the four categories on the O.H.P. transparency 'Why?'. Note that, although they bear a close resemblance to the Attainment Targets of the National Curriculum, they are not the same and are used in this instance to offer a wider vista of education. Indicate that, in this workshop, they will help colleagues to select objectives speedily thus leaving more time to work on the more important issue of selecting the activities.

Implementation — 60 to 75 minutes

1. Workshop — 30 to 45 minutes — small groups
    As you move from group to group, clarify that the objective number of their choice should be entered in the box provided, where, for a particular developmental stage, no objective is given, they are free to use one of their own creation. Try to get them to think of a different activity for each objective whilst making the point that many objectives can be worked towards through a simple task.

2. Discussion — 30+ minutes — whole group
   Using the OHP's prepared during the workshop, ask each group to share their thinking. Finally, reveal the source of the objectives (see below) to make the point that a number of curriculum areas can have similar objectives. For example, the skill of problem solving is equally important to Mathematics and the Humanities; indeed, it is a life skill.

   Schools' Council Publications: source of objectives
   Science 5–13
   Place, Time and Society
   Religious Education 5–13
   Home and Family

TOPIC...
STAGE ....

Objective number			Activity
SKILLS	Social		
	Physical		
	Intellectual		
	Investigative		
	Designing and making		
PERSONAL QUALITIES	Attitudes		
	Values & interests		
	Emotional		
CONCEPTS			
KNOWLEDGE			

Working Objectively

Workshop 2: Planning a Topic Objectively

1. Workshop — Work in small groups.
   1.1 Choose a topic which motivates the group as a whole and decide upon a particular target population, i.e. developmental stage of pupil (1a, 1b, 2 or 3).
   1.2 Now, using the attached list of objectives arranged according to developmental stage, select those objectives which it would be appropriate to work towards through the topic adopted.
   1.3 Indicate, on the table, the objective selected and the activities you would use to achieve them. Transfer to the O.H.P. provided.
2. Discussion

OBJECTIVES

STAGE 1a (Age 5–7 on average)

SKILLS	Social	

SKILLS   Social
1. The ability to participate within small groups
2. Participate effectively in a group activity
3. Practice necessary social skills, e.g. talking to friends, thinking about and helping other people, developing tolerance, adaptability and flexibility

Physical
1. The ability to manipulate equipment
2. The ability to manipulate equipment to find and communicate information
3. The ability to explore the expressive powers of the human body to communicate ideas and feelings
4. Carry out manipulative tasks to facilitate development of hand/eye coordination?
5. Practise a variety of manipulative tasks to develop motor skills involving movement of the hands, fingers and forearm

Intellectual
1. Ability to group things consistently according to chosen or given criteria
2. Ability to use displayed reference material for identifying living and non-living things
3. Ability to record events in their sequences
4. Ability to use representational symbols for recording information on charts of block graphs
5. The ability to find information from a variety of sources, in a variety of ways
6. The ability to communicate findings through an appropriate medium
7. Master new words

	Investigative	1. Ability to find answers to simple problems by investigation
		2. Ability to make comparisons in terms of one property or variable
		3. Awareness of cause–effect relationships
		4. Develop greater awareness of objectives and materials through the sense organs
		5. Explore new problems posed through concrete examples
		6. Observe, experiment and discover
		7. Test new ideas for themselves
PERSONAL QUALITIES	Attitudes	1. Sensitivity to the need for giving proper care to living things
		2. Enjoyment in using all the senses for exploring and discriminating
		3. Willingness to collect material for observation or investigation
		4. The fostering of curiosity through the encouragement of questions
	Values and Interests	
	Emotional	1. Experience the satisfaction which comes with the successful completions of an activity
CONCEPTS		
KNOWLEDGE		1. Appreciation of the variety of living things and materials in the environment
		2. Awareness of changes which take place as time passes
		3. Recognition of common shapes — square, circle, triangle
		4. Recognition of regularity in patterns
		5. Awareness of the meaning of words which describe various types of quantity
		6. Appreciation that things which are different may have features in common
		7. Awareness of the properties which materials can have
		8. Knowledge of religion in the locality e.g. buildings, people, activities

OBJECTIVES

STAGE 1b (Age 7–9 on average)

SKILLS	Social	1. Willing participation in group work
		2. Develop greater awareness of relationships
		3. Develop interest in other countries and people
		4. Develop further their concept of 'family'?

	Physical	1. Skill in manipulating tools and materials
		2. Development of techniques for handling living things correctly
		3. Ability to record impressions by making models, painting or drawing

	Intellectual	1. Willing compliance with safety regulations in handling tools and equipment
		2. Awareness that there are various ways of expressing results and observations
		3. Recognition of the action of force
		4. Ability to distinguish regularity in events and motion
		5. Ability to tabulate information and use tables
		6. Verbalize ideas and problems, e.g. asking questions as well as answering them
		7. Use tables of content and index
		8. Use a dictionary
		9. Collect and classify
		10. Use books to find information

	Investigative	1. Awareness that there are various ways of testing out ideas and making observations
		2. Appreciation of the need for measurement
		3. Awareness that more than one variable may be involved in a particular change

PERSONAL QUALITIES	Attitudes	1. Desire to find out things for oneself
		2. Willingness to wait and to keep records in order to observe change in things

	Values and Interests	1. Interest in discussing and comparing the aesthetic qualities of materials
		2. Development of an artistic response.

	Emotional	1. Enjoyment in comparing measurements with estimates
		2. Prepare for the physiological changes which come with adolescence?

CONCEPTS	1. Formation of the notions of the horizontal and the vertical
	2. Development of concepts of conservation of length and substance
	3. Awareness of the meaning of speed and of its relation to distance covered
	4. Appreciation that ability to move or cause movement requires energy
	5. Development of a concept of environment
	6. Concept of festivals and celebration e.g. Christmas, Divali, Eid-ul-Fitr
KNOWLEDGE	1. Awareness of change of living things and non-living materials
	2. Familiarity with sources of sound
	3. Awareness of sources of heat, light and electricity
	4. Appreciation of man's use of other living things and their products
	5. Awareness that man's way of life has changed through the ages
	6. Awareness of seasonal changes in living things
	7. Awareness of differences in physical conditions between different parts of the Earth
	8. Appreciation that properties of materials influence their use
	9. Knowledge of sacred literature, ways of conveying meaning: myth, symbol, ritual

OBJECTIVES

STAGE 2 (Age 9–11 on average)

SKILLS	Social	1. Willingness to co-operate with others in science activities
		2. An awareness of significant groups within the community and the wider society
		3. A developing understanding of how individuals relate to such groups
		4. A willingness to consider participating constructively in the activities associated with these groups
		5. Exploration of self and others belonging: family homes, community, harmony
		6. Develop their social awareness, e.g. games can be useful in teaching them to keep to the rules and respect the rights of others
		7. Work out a satisfactory self-image in relation to their family, friends and community?

Physical		1. Skill in devising and constructing simple apparatus
		2. Develop fine specialized skills from basic manipulative movements?
Intellectual		1. Preference for putting ideas to test before accepting or rejecting them
		2. Ability to construct and use keys for identification
		3. Awareness of symmetry in shapes and structures
		4. Ability to frame questions likely to be answered through investigations
		5. Ability to choose and use either arbitrary or standard units of measurement as appropriate
		6. Awareness of sequences of change in natural phenomena
		7. Awareness of structure-function relationship in parts of living things
		8. Appreciation of the relationships of parts and wholes
		9. Awareness that many factors need to be considered when choosing a material for a particular use
		10. The ability to interpret pictures, charts, graphs, map, etc.
		11. Capacity to conveying meanings: myth, ritual
		12. Identify, memorize, selectively recall and use important facts
		13. Seriate familar items
		14. Choose appropriate ways of communicating results of their work to others, e.g. oral, graphic, pictorial and written modes of presentation
		15. Obtain information from a variety of sources (The teacher must help the pupil to develop library techniques, e.g. to recognize information, to discriminate between information and propaganda, to skim)
		16. Understand the changes that are beginning to take place in their bodies?

Physical

1. Skill in devising and constructing simple apparatus
2. Develop fine specialized skills from basic manipulative movements?

Intellectual

1. Preference for putting ideas to test before accepting or rejecting them
2. Ability to construct and use keys for identification
3. Awareness of symmetry in shapes and structures
4. Ability to frame questions likely to be answered through investigations
5. Ability to choose and use either arbitrary or standard units of measurement as appropriate
6. Awareness of sequences of change in natural phenomena
7. Awareness of structure-function relationship in parts of living things
8. Appreciation of the relationships of parts and wholes
9. Awareness that many factors need to be considered when choosing a material for a particular use
10. The ability to interpret pictures, charts, graphs, map, etc.
11. Capacity to conveying meanings: myth, ritual
12. Identify, memorize, selectively recall and use important facts
13. Seriate familar items
14. Choose appropriate ways of communicating results of their work to others, e.g. oral, graphic, pictorial and written modes of presentation
15. Obtain information from a variety of sources (The teacher must help the pupil to develop library techniques, e.g. to recognize information, to discriminate between information and propaganda, to skim)
16. Understand the changes that are beginning to take place in their bodies?

Investigative

1. Willingness to observe objectively
2. Ability to classify living things and non-living materials in different ways
3. Test ideas and solve problems bearing in mind one variable at a time
4. Collect and classify information, drawing out significant features?

PERSONAL QUALITIES

Attitudes

1. Willingness to assume responsibility for the proper care of living things
2. Willingness to examine critically the results for their own and others' work
3. Talk and listen to adults?

<table>
<tr><td>Values and Interests</td><td>

1. Appreciation of the reasons for safety regulations
2. Interest in choosing suitable means of expressing results and observations
3. Develop their interest in the growth and development of young children
</td></tr>
<tr><td>Emotional</td><td>

1. Enjoyment in developing methods for solving problems or testing ideas
2. Appreciation of the part that aesthetic qualities of materials play in determining their use
3. Exploration of self identity, power, sense, feelings
4. Be reassured about the normality of their development
</td></tr>
</table>

CONCEPTS

1. Appreciation that comparisons can be made indirectly by use of an intermediary
2. Development of concepts of conservation of weight, area and volume
3. Understanding of the speed, time distance relation

KNOWLEDGE

1. Familiarity with a wide range of forces and of ways in which they can be changed
2. Knowledge of the origins of common materials
3. Awareness of changes in the design of measuring instruments and tools during man's history
4. Awareness of the changes in the physical environment brought about by man's activity
5. Appreciation of how the form and structure of materials relate to their function and properties
6. Knowledge of founders of religion e.g. Christ past and present
7. Gain knowledge of tools appropriate to the performance of various manipulative tasks?

OBJECTIVES

STAGE 3 (Age 11+ on average)

SKILLS   Social

1. Appreciation of the social implications of the human race's changing use of materials, historical and contemporary
2. Appreciation of the role of science in the changing pattern of provision for human needs
3. Consider how other people behave within groups and the reasons for different patterns of behaviour

Physical

1. The ability to plan and execute expressive activities to communicate ideas and feelings
2. Become more efficient in performing manipulative tasks

Intellectual
1. Ability to apply relevant knowledge without help of contextual cues
2. Ability to select the graphical form most appropriate to the information being recorded
3. Ability to deduce information from graphs: from gradient, area, intercept
4. The ability to organize information through concepts and generalizations
5. Organizing knowledge: truth and meaning
6. Language skills: metaphor, symbol

Investigative
1. Preference for choosing the most appropriate means of expressing results or observations
2. Appreciation that classification criteria are arbitrary
3. Ability to separate, exclude or combine variables in appreciating problems
4. Ability to extend reasoning beyond the actual to the possible
5. Ability to construct scale models for investigation and to appreciate implications of changing the scale
6. Ability to draw from observations conclusions that are unbiased by preconception
7. Awareness that the degree of accuracy of measurements has to be taken into account when results are interpreted
8. Willingness to check that conclusions are consistent with further evidence
9. The ability to evaluate information
10. The ability to formulate and test hypotheses and generalizations
11. Devise techniques of analysis appropriate to given situations
12. Formulate generalizations and test hypotheses
13. Examine evidence critically, evaluate information and draw conclusions
14. Review previous conclusions in the light of new factual knowledge
15. Express ideas, observations and conclusions in appropriate ways
16. Develop the ability to plan ahead
17. Read widely

PERSONAL
1. Preference for using words correctly
2. Recognition of the needs to acquire new skills
3. Willingness to extend methods used in science activities to other fields of experience
4. The fostering of a willingness to explore personal attitudes and values to relate these to other people's

5. The encouraging of an openness to the possibility of change in attitudes and values
6. The encouragement of worthwhile and developing interests in human affairs
7. Development of open questioning reflective attitude
8. Development of commitment to search for meaning

Values and Interests

1. Development of interest in different ways of looking at life

Emotional

1. The ability to exercise empathy (i.e. the capacity to imagine accurately what it might be like to be someone else)
2. Accept physical changes that are occurring in their bodies at different times and at different rates
3. Develop a favourable self-image through group activities
4. Explore their expressive powers to communicate ideas and feelings
5. Develop an understanding of the opposite sex through reading, discussion, role playing, etc
6. Exploration of self and natural world — complexity, unity — birth, death, suffering, beauty, mystery — elements, light, darkness — humans in relation to natural world
7. Development of respect, sympathy for those having different views

CONCEPTS

1. Development of the concept of an internal environment
2. Appreciation of the scale of the universe
3. Recognition that energy has many forms and is conserved when it is changed from one form to another
4. Ideas of ultimate reality e.g. images and ideas about God

KNOWLEDGE

1. Familiarity with relationships involving velocity, distance, time, acceleration
2. Knowledge that chemical change results from interaction
3. Knowledge that energy can be stored and converted in various ways
4. Knowledge that properties of matter can be explained by reference to its particulate nature
5. Knowledge of certain properties of heat, light, sound, electrical, mechanical and chemical energy

Action Tactics 1: Implementing Programmes of Study

Workshop 1: Development of a Theme

Leader's Guide

You will need to select and resource five activities concerned with the theme of 'Movement'. The purpose of this session is to show how the theme of 'Movement' can be developed and extended by the use of cross curricular practical activities. Each is used to simultaneously develop Attainment Targets (at levels 1–3) in Maths, English and Science and many have been further augmented with linked work. In order to ensure to work towards each of the large number of Attainment Targets in the core curriculum alone, it is important to realize that activities can be used in this multifaceted way. It is the intention that the development of this theme of 'Movement' can be used by schools as a model upon which to base the implementation of the National Curriculum using a variety of other themes. You will find that 'Learning through Science' is a useful resource.

Introduction — 5 Minutes — Whole group

Put over the points made in the box below:

> Now it's your turn to have some fun! So that we can see how one activity might be used to develop not only Maths and English but also Science, it is useful to experience it at first hand. There are five sets of activities available to you, each of which develops the theme of 'Movement', and I would like you to choose one at which to work in groups of about three but no more than four people. Please keep notes of relevant points of your discussion as this will help, when we focus on the attainment targets. Remember that the overall objective is to develop this theme with your children in mind.
>
> A teacher's guide and pupil workcard (where appropriate) is provided for each, together with most of the equipment you will need, *now over to you!*

Implementation — 65 Minutes — Five groups of about three people

1. 'Hands on' experience of activities — 45 Minutes — small groups
   As you move round the groups you will need to make sure that they are aware of the nature of the task. Also, it is important that they work as a group, starting with the main activity, and do not divide up the work. Many sets of activities are sequenced and it is essential to be aware of this. Also it is crucial that everyone has the opportunity to experience all aspects of the activities (Maths, Science and English) if the Cross Curricular nature of the theme is to be fully understood.

2. Development of ideas — 20 Minutes — small groups
   When you are sure that each set of activities has been completed and appropriate records have been made, participants can be invited to think of other ideas to develop the theme further.

Plenary — 5 Minutes — whole group

It is important to put over the idea that participants now have five sets of activities each of which have been further developed and which can be used with children and that they are now beginning to build up an important Cross Curricular resource for use in school. Secondly, the point made earlier that the development of the theme of 'Movement' is exemplar should be emphasized.

Implementing Programmes of Study

Workshop 1: Development of a Theme

Work in small groups of about 3 people

1. 'Hands on' experience of activities
   Five sets of activities are provided all concerned with the theme of 'Movement'!

   Choose one of these only and work through the activity, making a record as you go along. Each set has a Teacher's Guide and Pupil Workcard (as appropriate) to help you.

   It is important that you work as a group and do not divide up the tasks. Also, many of the sets of activities are sequenced, so you need to start at the beginning and work through each in turn.

2. Development of ideas
   Now get together and develop other activities which explore the same theme. If you prefer, think of other areas such as 'Movement on land', 'Movement in the air' or 'Movement on water'.

Action Tactics 1: Implementing Programmes of Study

Workshop 2: Familiarization with Attainment Targets

Leader's Guide

The purpose here is to give participants the experience of matching appropriate Attainment Targets to children's activities. It will also help them to become familiar with the range of targets in Maths, Science and English in Key Stage 1 and reassure them that the National Curriculum can, in practice, be implemented through thematic work.

Introduction — 2 Minutes — Whole group

Put over the points made in the box below:

So, how can we relate these Attainment Targets to what actually goes on in the classroom? Perhaps, the best way is to start with the children and the activities which we might provide for them linked, in this instance, to the theme of 'Movement'. You may well be surprised at the number and range of A.Ts that are being included in the kind of work that you are already doing!

Implementation — 28 Minutes — Five groups of about three people (the same groups as in the last workshop).

The workshop involves matching Attainment Targets, at specific levels, to the main activity carried out by the group.

1. 20 minutes allowed
2. 6 minutes allowed
3. 2 minutes allowed

Workshop 2: Familiarization with Attainment Targets

Work in small groups
Have the Statements of Attainment (for a particular Key Stage) available in Mathematics, Science and English.

1. Work as a group
   Firstly, select a Key Stage within which to work.

   Now work through each of the Statements of Attainment in turn, discussing, as a group, whether they apply to the activity (on the theme of 'Movement') already undertaken. Make a list of those that are being worked towards through the activity.
2. In the same groups
   Discuss the findings of the selection activity which you have just completed.

   Which Statements of Attainment have been missed out?

   Can you think of other activities within the theme of 'Movement' through which they could be approached or would you need to achieve balance through the selection of another theme?
3. Whole group discussion
   Are some themes more productive than others in terms of the Core Curriculum and, if so, how can we best select them?

Action Tactics 1: Finding Out About Resources

Workshop 1: The School Site — Maximizing the potential of the school environment

Leader's Guide

With falling roles and meagre resources it is becoming all the more important to realize the potential of the close environs of the school — in particular the immediate locality, but more importantly the site itself, even though, on the surface, it has little to offer other than the tarmac surface of the playgound.

This workshop provides help in allowing colleagues to explore the potential of their own school site as a group exercise. You will need to obtain the videotape 'Outside In' from the Department of Education and Science.

Introduction — 5 Minutes — whole group

Put over the points made in the box below:

Now we are unable to finance the number of school visits enjoyed in the past, we must make a determined effort to maximize the potential of our own school environment. Using the school site had many advantages; two immediately spring to mind, it is cheap and 'on the doorstep' which means that the time and cost of travel can be ignored. Surely, however poor its potential appears to be, its development is worth considering for these reasons alone.

Implementation — 75 minutes

1. Workshop
   1.1 Viewing the videotape 'Outside In' — 25 minutes — whole group
        Make the comment that, although the film was made some time ago, the message it carries is as relevant today as it was when it was made. Show the film which is about the transformation of theory into practice in Kent.
   1.2 Working objectively — 20 minutes — whole group
        Ask colleagues to work out a set of objectives which would be appropriate to the development of their own school site for environmental science work.
   1.3 Developing the site — 15 minutes — whole group
        What particular developments would be needed to work towards the objectives identified? Ask colleagues to consider this question.
2. Discussion — 'Identifying priorities' — 15 minutes — whole group
   Development costs time and money! Clearly the facilities the school intends to provide cannot materialize all at once; ask colleagues now to decide upon their priorities and work out a plan of action over an appropriate time scale.
3. Conclusion 'formalizing the plans'
   Select one member of staff to mark in the agreed developments on a plan of your own school, indicating for each, the time scale suggested.

Finding out About Resources

Workshop 1: The School Site — *Maximizing* the potential of the school environment

How much do *you* use your own school site? This workshop allows you to explore its potential and to discuss ways in which it might be developed for educational purposes.

1. Workshop
   1.1 Viewing the film 'Outside In'
       As you watch the film, identify those issues which are most relevant to your own situation.
   1.2 Working objectively
       Work in small groups and compile a list of objectives which would be relevant to the development of your own school site.
   1.3 Developing the site
       Now join together in a large group and combine lists of objectives. Identify the particular developments which would be needed to work towards the list of objectives compiled.
2. Discussion — 'Identifying priorities'
   As a group, decide upon your priorities and work out a plan of action over an appropriate time scale. Record your views on the attached sheet.
3. Conclusion — 'Formalizing the Plans'
   Ask for a volunteer who would be prepared to mark in the agreed developments on a plan of the school and oversee progress according to the time scale envisaged.

TIME SCALE	PLAN OF ACTION

Action Tactics 1: Finding out About Resources

Workshop 2: Curriculum Development Projects — An evaluation

Leader's Guide

When trying to bring about change in a school, it is important that any steps taken are not too large for the individual teachers concerned; each must feel confident about incorporating the projected change within his or her current practice. As a curricular developer, it is important that you know where individual teachers are with respect to their science and design technology teaching; this is particularly important when considering which pupil/teacher materials are appropriate for the school. Although particular projects would seem to match the needs of the children admirably, unless they also meet the needs of the teacher, they will remain, unopened, on the staffroom shelf.

With this in mind, it is useful to set up a situation which allows your colleagues to evaluate a whole selection of materials, preferably before purchase. *At this stage, you must allow them some freedom of choice, whilst being aware, at the same time, that their views may change as their confidence grows.* Such an anticipated change may well bring financial problems with it, however, the advice still holds and is important in terms of initiating science and technology teaching in the school.

Introduction — 5 minutes — whole group

Put over the points made in the box below:

> So that we do not buy a 'pig in a poke' I have borrowed a number of pupil/teacher materials for us to look at. The Teachers' Centre is happy for us to keep them for another week so I'm going to suggest that we divide them between us and report back next week.

Implementation

1. Workshop — During the week in colleague's own time — in pairs or threes
   Ask teachers to choose a project and evaluate it with respect to target population (the type of child), aims and objectives, the style of workcard and so on. *Make sure that everyone looks at all the materials during the week, if only briefly.* See that they pay particular attention to whether the material is prescriptive or open ended and whether the level is appropriate for the expected range of development in the age range specified. *Provide your colleagues with guidelines* (e.g. the 'Sussex Scheme' 'Framework for Analysis of Curriculum Materials' P. 234/E 364 The Open University) *should they wish to use them.*
2. Discussion — 60 minutes — whole group
   Ask each group to give their evaluation of the chosen project.
3. Conclusion — 30 minutes — whole group
   Try to lead colleagues toward making a decision about which materials to purchase.

   It may well be that the staff settles for a variety of materials; the choice may be determined by individual preferences, the nature of the topics currently taught in the school and so on. Whatever the outcome, try to ensure that the materials match the needs of both teachers and children.

Finding out About Resources

Workshop 2: Curriculum Development Projects — An Evaluation

Are *you* familiar with all the teacher/pupil materials that are currently available? Have you had the time to evaluate those that you are aware of? By borrowing a range of materials and dividing the work between colleagues, the task is made easier and we are less likely to waste our money on unsuitable projects.

1. Workshop
    First, choose a project and a colleague with whom to work. Between you, during the week, try to make some evaluation of the materials chosen; guidelines are available if you wish to use them or you can agree on criteria within the group if you prefer. However, make sure you have something prepared for the report session next week.
2. Discussion
    After listening to the evaluation of all the projects selected, you will now be in a position to come to a decision regarding the materials which would be suitable for use in *your* school.

Action Tactics 1: Being Familiar with Safety Matters

Workshop 1: Safety Quiz

Leader's guide

Traditionally certain practices have been acceptable in primary schools and, until recently, little thought has been given to their desirability or, indeed, the safety hazards introduced. Furthermore, other issues have also been clarified, one of these being the designation of responsibilities. By and large most class teachers are unaware of the new safety measures which should be taken and, certainly, have had too little time to keep themselves informed. The purpose of this workshop is to highlight, for them, the most important issues.

Introduction — 5 minutes — whole group

Put over the points made in the box below:

> The other day one of my children brought in a dead shrew. He was absolutely fascinated by its long nose and how small it was. Also, how it had come to be dead and when it had happened. Of course, I was anxious to use the experience to advantage so I . . . . What would you have done in this circumstance? Perhaps this workshop will help you find an answer!)

Implementation — 55 minutes

1. Workshop — Safety Quiz — 25 minutes — in pairs
    You will need to provide considerable support during this workshop since it raises issues which may not have been questioned previously and for which an established, but not necessarily safe, code of practice has been in operation for some time.
2. Discussion — Safety Quiz — 30 minutes — whole group
    Take each of the points in turn and ask for comment from the groups. Be quite sure that, for each, you make the approved, safe course of action extremely clear.

Being Familiar with Safety Matters

Workshop 1: Safety Quiz

What safety measures do you take in your classroom? You know about the first-aid box and the need to report accidents, but what should you know about keeping gerbils or cutting plastics? This workshop is designed to help you find out about these and other issues to do with classroom safety.

1. Workshop — Safety Quiz
    Work through the quiz in pairs trying to come to some agreement in making a response. You may use the reference books provided if necessary.
2. Discussion — Safety Quiz
    What do we need to know about classroom/school safety?

You will find the ASE publication, 'Be Safe' of value here.

Safety Quiz

We will use this quiz as the basis for discussions about safety in our science and design technology teaching. No attempt has been made to give the questions any pattern of priority.

1. You have made some bacteriological and fungal cultures for your classes. How should you dispose of these? What dangers do you see in cultivating micro-organisms?
2. How could you protect pupils from contacting microbiological material?
3. If an animal (e.g. gerbil, hamster) bites a child, what should you do? What precautions can you take to ensure that the animals do not bite?
4. Make a list of six dangerous plants, which could be brought into school by pupils. Try to state the main source of danger in each case (e.g. seed).
5. Whose responsibility is it to see that your electrical equipment is correctly wired? Do you check it regularly?
6. Do you have a first-aid box available? Where is it?
7. Itemize possible hazards in your own classroom.
8. At what age (development stage) do you feel that children can safely handle tools, such as saws and hammers?
9. What dangers could arise if you have a colour-blind child in your class?
10. What precautions do you consider are necessary when asking children to use themselves as subjects?
11. Suppose you were using a small source of heat, such as a spirit lamp, and you knocked it over causing a small fire. You try to extinguish the fire with an extinguisher, but it is empty. Whose responsibility is it in a school to ensure that fire extinguishers work properly?
12. Is it wise to bring in British wild animals into the classroom? If not, why not?
13. What routine should you establish in looking after animals' cages?
14. When children have handled animals or cages, what should they do?
15. How much should you allow children to taste substances in experiments?

16. Does your school have a written safety policy?
17. Do you consider that safety problems are given the same priority as other school acti-
    vities?
18. At what age (development stage) should you allow children to use glue guns?
19. Is a shaper saw suitable for children to use? If so, why and at what stage?

Action Tactics 1: Being Familiar with Safety Matters

Workshop 2: Safety Matters

Leader's Guide

At some stage it is desirable for children to work in a science laboratory. Clearly, in this situation, additional safety hazards may well be introduced. What steps do we, as teachers, take to circumvent accidents? This workshop is designed to allow colleagues to explore a pack of materials which allow children to make decisions about the safe control of their own environment.

Introduction — 5 minutes — whole group

Put over the points made in the box below:

> I'm sure that most of you are very concerned about laboratory safety! I know that some of you take children through a list of do's and don'ts which you have built into your programmes. How much do you think the children take in when this approach is used? How relevant, at the time, is it? Is there a better way? The workshop allows you to explore this issue through the use of materials which allow the pupils to make their own informal discussions about laboratory safety.

Implementation — 70 minutes
1. Workshop 'Safety Matters', obtainable from Phillip Harris Ltd, Lynn Lane, Shenstone, Staffordshire WS14 DEE — small group
   Set the workshop out, as a circus, in four stations entitled:
   (a) 'Writing Simple Rules'
   (b) 'Expanding the Rules' (Safety Handouts)
   (c) 'Safety In Action' (Safety Test)
   (d) Crossword, Quizword, Wordsearch, Game 2. Safety Checklist:
       'How Safe is Your Laboratory?' Case Studies
   You will need to make sure that the appropriate AVA equipment is also available. Distribute the work between four groups if possible.
2. Discussion — 'Safety Matters' — 40 Minutes — whole group
   Ask each group, in turn, to describe and evaluate the activities in their section. Also allow time for questions during each input.

Being Familiar with Safety Matters

Workshop 2: Safety Matters

How familiar are older children with the safety precautions they should take, particularly when they are working in a laboratory? This workshop allows you to explore a pack of materials which you can then use with children.

1. Workshop — 'Safety Matters'
    The workshop has been set out in four stations. In groups of two or three, review as many of the materials as possible.
2. Discussion — 'Safety Matters'
    As a group, review each of the suggested activities and evaluate their possible effectiveness as teaching material.

Discussion Tactics 2

Discussion Tactics 2: Formulating a School Policy

Workshop 1: Policy versus Syllabus

Leader's Guide

A 'Nominal Group Technique' may be used as a method for obtaining group responses to problems which:

- (i) ensures that *everyone* contributes,
- (ii) avoids the dominance of the group by a few people with strong ideas,
- (iii) avoids too narrow an interpretation of the task,
- (iv) ensures a wide variety of responses,
- (v) allows a systematic ordering of priorities.

Introduction — 10 minutes — small group

Task presentation
The task, or question is written on the blackboard or overhead projector, e.g. *What are the major advantages of formulating a policy rather than a syllabus for science and/or design technology in school?*

Task clarification
A shared understanding of the question is essential. Spend time in group discussion to ensure that everyone understands the nature of the task.

Implementation — 50 minutes

1. Workshop — 40 minutes — small groups
   1.1 *Silent nominations*
       Individuals list their own private responses (at least 10 minutes).
   1.2 *Personal ranking*
       Individuals then rank their own list to establish felt priorities.
   1.3 *Master list*
       Leaders compile a master list on the blackboard or overhead projector taking *one* item from each group member in rotation. No editing of material is allowed and no evaluative comments are to be made at this stage. It will be helpful to number items.

1.4 *Item clarification*

In this phase each item is discussed until all members know what it means. Clarification only is allowed. If a member of the group now feels that their item is already covered by someone else's, they may request its withdrawal. No pressure should be applied to any individual to have items withdrawn or incorporated in another.

1.5 *Evaluation*

It is now necessary to decide the relative importance of items in the eyes of the group. Each person is allowed *five* weighted votes (five points for the point that is felt to be most important, four points for the next etc.) A simple voting procedure allows the consensus to emerge.

2. Discussion — 10 minutes — whole group

Discussion/action

Now that the composite picture has emerged, more general group discussions can proceed.

Reminders to Group Leaders

(1) Do not reinterpret a person's ideas.
(2) Use the participant's own wording.
(3) Do not interject your own ideas — *you are not participating*.
(4) Give people time to think.
(5) This is *not* a debate — do not allow participants to challenge each other or attempt to persuade each other.
(6) Do not try to interpret results — do not look for patterns.

Formulating a School Policy

Workshop 1: Policy versus Syllabus

Have *you* ever tried to analyze the difference between a policy and a syllabus? Have you considered which might be best? This workshop allows you to consider these issues as individuals and then come to an agreement, as a staff, about which to adopt.

1. Workshop
   1.1 Individually, list your own private response to the question 'What are the major advantages of formulating a policy rather than a syllabus for Science and/or Design Technology in school?'
   1.2 Now rank your list in order of priority, so that the most important point appears at the top of the list.
   1.3 As a group, compile a master list.
   1.4 Item clarification.
   1.5 Evaluation of items. You will be allowed to choose five items from the list and allot points to each, five points for the most important and so on.
2. Discussion.

Action Tactics 2

Action Tactics 2: Assessing Children's Science and Design Technology Level

Workshop 1: Introducing a Criterion-Referenced Checklist

Leader's Guide

If we are to match the activities we provide for children to the developmental level of individuals, then we need a reliable method of finding out where each child is in his or her thinking. One such method is to use a criterion-referenced check list against which to make a judgment which, for the most part, is used to help us make an immediate response through our teaching. Used over a much longer period of time (say, at least a term) on a number of occasions and in a variety of circumstances, such a check list can be used to construct a pupil profile which may be used as a permanent record of progress.

This activity introduces the use of such a check list and provides an opportunity for colleagues to familiarize themselves with it.

Introduction — 5 minutes — whole group.

Put over the points made in the box below:

> I am sure that you are all familiar with the use of the term 'reading age', but why can't we also talk of 'science level'? In this session we are going to explore a way of finding this out using a check list derived from those Statements of Attainment in Science A.T.1 concerned with investigation, but, first, I want you to enjoy yourselves by making and investigating tops!

Identify the source of the workcard ('Learning through Science: Coloured things': 'Spinning Colour' Macdonald Educational Press) and stress the importance of working at their own level i.e. that of an adult.

At this stage do not allow discussion about the way in which children would react.

Implementation — 55 minutes

1. Workshop — 30 minutes — Groups of two or three
   Allow this to progress for long enough to be satisfying. Cutting the time limit for this particular activity can be frustrating and thus counter-productive. Try to obtain feedback from all the groups fairly frequently so that you are in a position to identify the groups upon which you will base your discussion.

2. Discussion — 25 minutes — whole group
    Ask for feedback from the groups, regarding the level at which they were working judged against the Statements of Attainment concerned with investigation. Be positive in whom you ask. You should try to highlight stages in the acquisition of process skills and use the discussion to introduce the investigation column on the checklist. Try to put over to the group the *progression* of skills acquisition involved, and give some indication of questions to ask of children e.g. is that 'fair'? are you sure? can you think of another way to find out? etc.

Assessing Children's Science and Design Technology Level

Workshop 1: Introducing a Criterion-Referenced Checklist

If we are to provide appropriate activities for children, then we must be sure of where they are in their thinking. This workshop provides you with a method of ascertaining this which is much less subjective than others you may have used previously.

1. Workshop — Problem solving — 'Tip Top'
    Work in small groups, decide upon an approach (you may ask for extra equipment and materials if you wish within reason) and implement it. Make a careful record of your results and the methods/s used.
2. Discussion
    The progression of Investigative Skills with increasing maturity based upon some of the Statements of Attainment in the Science A.T. 1. (see below).

A.T. 1 Exploration of Science: Statements of Attainment:
Checklist of investigative skills.

Investigation
2.1. Ask questions and suggest ideas of the 'how and why' variety.
2.2. Identify and describe simple differences such as hot/cold, rough/smooth.
3.1. Formulate hypotheses. For example 'this ball will bounce higher than that one'.
3.2. Identify and describe simple variables that change over time, such as growth of a plant.
3.3. Distinguish between 'fair' and 'unfair' tests.
4.1. Raise questions in a form which can be investigated.
4.2. Plan an investigation where the plan indicates that the relevant variables have been identified and others controlled.
4.3. Formulate a testable hypothesis.
4.4. Construct 'fair tests'.
4.5. Carry out an investigation with due regard to safety.
5.1. Use concepts, knowledge and skills to suggest simple questions and design investigations to answer them.
5.2. Identify and manipulate relevant independent and dependent variables choosing appropriately between ranges, numbers and values.

Key: 2.1 = National Curriculum Level 2, Attribute 1

Action Tactics 2: Assessing Children's Science and Design Technology Level

Workshop 2: Using a Criterion-Referenced Checklist

Leader's Guide

It is expected that any school science and design technology curriculum should allow for progression of pupils, both within and between classes. If such an idea is to operate effectively, it is crucial that teachers are aware of the level of development of each of the children in their care and that they can then select activities for each child which are appropriate for that level of development.

This workshop builds upon the previous one, 'Assessing the science level of children' and provides another opportunity for teachers to familiarize themselves with and use the 'Checklist of Investigative Skills' which it introduced.

Introduction — 5 minutes — whole group

Put over the points made in the box below:

> Now we're going to have some fun! As you can see, I have some bags, containing selections of balls, stop clocks and metre rules. Preferably I would like you to work in pairs, certainly no more than three in a group and find out which of the balls in your bag is the best bouncer; then put them in order.

Implementation — 70 minutes

1. Workshop — 30 minutes — small groups
    In making up the bags of balls you should be careful to include a ball of plasticene, some which behave in a way that you wouldn't expect, a 'miracle bouncer, some which are hollow, 'holey' and solid, and, as well as some which are large/small, a number which are of the same size/material/structure so that one variable, at least, may be controlled to some extent. *The overall success of this activity very much depends upon the care with which you make up the sets of balls.*

    While the activity is in progress, observe each group closely, look for the following:
    a. the criterion used to determine the best bouncer: is time/number of bounces or height used?
    b. the science level at which individuals are working. Use the investigation column on the checklist for this; try to ascertain how many of the variables individuals are able to identify and how many they are attempting to control.
2. Discussion — 20 minutes — whole group
    First ask each group to 'rate' themselves with respect to the checklist, using the investigation column in particular, giving reasons for their choice of 'science level'.

    Not only should this cause some amusement, but also provide you with the opportunity to identify the variables involved (height of drop; method of initiating bounce; material; size; shape; colour; structure of ball; experimenter; bouncing surface and so on) with the group and discuss 'fair testing'.

    Undoubtedly some groups will have complicated the problem and tried to find re-lationships between, say, height of bounce and structure of the ball/size of ball/material of which the ball is made and so on. Clearly it would be very difficult to find reliable answers to these problems with the materials given but it does provide you with clues about the level of thinking of the investigator in question. This should also be discussed if relevant. *Stress that the observation of working methods becomes most important where children are concerned.* For example, are they using 'fair tests' to determine which of the balls, *in the group they are experimenting with*, is the best bouncer, or, are they wanting to know which factors are important when considering bouncing ability? When children reach this latter level of working, it becomes increasingly difficult to find answers using the 'everyday' materials that are available to most primary school teachers.

3. Videotape — Using the checklist — 15 minutes — whole group
   For this workshop you will need to have a videotape available upon which to base the work. This should feature contrasting groups (working at different levels) from a local school. It is preferable to record groups working within the whole class: ten minutes of edited tape will be ample. Collect records of the children's work for discussion purposes.

   View the videotape a group at a time and ask those involved to assess the level of working of the children; their records of work will be of some help here.

   Try to bring out the differences between the groups and individual children working within a group. Use the childrens' records of their work to advantage when discussing ways of collecting information about the level at which an individual child operates. Such evidence can be contrasted with other observations gleamed from watching, listening, questioning and conversing with children.

4. Conclusion — Assessing Children's 'Science Level' — 5 minutes — whole group.

Exploration of Science: Statements of Attainment:

A Criterion-Referenced Checklist

Level	Observation	Investigation	Communication	Interpretation
1	Observe familiar materials and events in their environment at first-hand using their senses.		Describe and communicate their observations, ideally through talking in groups or by other means within their class.	
2	1. List and collate observations. 2. Use non-standard and standard measures	1. Ask questions and suggest ideas of the "how and why" variety 2. Identify and describe simple differences such as hot/cold, rough/smooth.	Record findings in charts, drawings and other appropriate forms.	Interpret findings by associating one factor with another, such as light objects float.
Av. 7 yrs.				
3	1. Select and use simple instruments to enhance observations e.g. stopclock or handlens. 2. Quantify variables as appropriate to the nearest labelled division of simple measuring instruments, such as a rule.	1. Formulate hypotheses for example, 'this ball will bounce higher than that one' 2. Identify and describe simple variables that change over time, such as growth of a plant. 3. Distinguish between a 'fair' and 'unfair' test.	1. Record findings in tables and bar charts. 2. Describe activities carried out by sequencing the major features.	1. Interpret simple pictograms and bar charts. 2. Interpret observations in terms of a generalized statement e.g. the greater the suspended weight, the longer the spring.

Level	Observation	Investigation	Communication	Interpretation
4 Av. 11 yrs.	Select and use a range of measuring instruments as appropriate to quantify observations of physical quantities, such as volume or temperature.	1. Raise questions in a form which can be investigated. 2. Plan an investigation where the plan indicates that the relevant variables have been identified and others controlled. 3. Formulate a testable hypothesis. 4. Construct 'fair tests'. 5. Carry out an investigation with due regard to safety.	1. Record results by appropriate means such as the construction of simple tables, bar charts, pie charts, line graphs 2. Describe investigations in the form of ordered prose, using a limited technical vocabulary. 3. Follow written instructions and diagramatic representations.	Draw conclusions from experimental results
5 Av. 14 yrs.	Select and use measuring instruments to quantify variables and use more complex measuring instruments with the required degree of accuracy, e.g. minor divisions on thermometers and forcemeters.	1. Use concepts, knowledge and skills to suggest simple questions and design investigations to answer them. 2. Identify and manipulate relevant independent and dependent variables choosing appropriately between ranges, numbers and values.	Make written statements of the patterns derived from the data obtained from various sources.	

Assessing Children's Science and Design Technology Level

Workshop 2: Using a Criterion-Referenced Checklist

Now that you are familiar with the checklist you are invited to attempt another problem yourself and then to consider the level of working of two groups of children attempting to solve the same problem.

1. Workshop
   You have been provided with a bag of balls all of which have been purchased locally and are, therefore, within the everyday experience of children. Try to find out which of them is the best bouncer; arrange them in order of best.
2. Discussion — Bouncing Balls.
3. Video — tape — Using the checklist
   Using the check list, 'A.T. 1 Exploration of Science; Statements of Attainment' try to assess the level of working of the two groups of children on the video tape. The records of two of the children involved are included to help you make your decisions.
4. Conclusion — Assessing Children's 'Science' level.

Action Tactics 2: Assessing Children's Science and Design Technology Level

Workshop 3: Assessing Children's Science and Design Technology Level

Leader's Guide

Traditionally teachers have mainly used written records of children's work to help them assess scientific ability. In design technology, the quality of the finished product has been used as a guide. This workshop is designed to invite teachers to consider whether the gathering of information about children by any one method alone will provide them with enough evidence upon which to make a judgment.

Introduction — 5 minutes — whole group

Put over the points made in the box below:

> Before I introduced you to the science list (Statements of Attainment for A.T. 1), how did most of you assess your children's science work? Be honest, did you assess it at all? If you did, perhaps you just marked their books. Today's workshop raises the issue of exactly *how* we use such a checklist both in our everyday teaching and in making a more permanent record of individuals' levels of development.

Implementation — 85 minutes — whole group

1. Slide/Tape Sequence — Classroom Observational Techniques — 20 minutes — whole group
    Use the sequence from *Match and Mismatch* (Oliver and Boyd) entitled 'What is Observing?' playing it straight through without comment. It is worth noting that many LEAs hold a copy of this publication centrally. Although it does not introduce any new ideas, it brings together the five most important ways of finding out about children's thinking; these are through dialogue, by listening, by watching, through questioning and by looking at the products of work.
2. Discussion — Assessing Children's Science and Design Technology Level — 10 minutes — whole group
    In the discussion it is important to stress that:
    (a) No one method is satisfactory on its own.
    (b) Observation of any one child should be made in a variety of circumstances and on a number of occasions.
    (c) Observations, for the most part, are used immediately for the benefit of the child without a written record being made.
    (d) A period of at least one term should elapse before observations are used to make a written record of achievement.
3. Follow up activity — 5 minutes — whole group
    Invite the group to try out the 'bouncing ball' activity with a group of children of their own choosing and report back at the next session.

Assessing Children's Science and Design Technology Level

Workshop 3: Assessing Children's Science and Design Technology Level

You are now invited to consider, in more detail, the way in which you might use a checklist (i.e. Statements of Attainment) in a real classroom situation. What information about the children will you need? How will you collect it?

1. Slide/Tape Sequence — Classroom observational techniques
2. Discussion — Assessing Children's Science and Design Technology Level
3. Follow up activity
   Using the information gained in this workshop, you are invited to try out the 'bouncing balls' activity on a small group of children of your own choosing. Try to observe them carefully and come prepared to report on your findings at the next session, using written work, tape recordings or notes of observations made to support what you have to say.

Action Tactics 2: Assessing Children's Science and Design Technology Level

Workshop 4: Designing and Assessing Activities

Leader's Guide

This workshop is designed to help you implement and assess particular Attainment Targets within the National Curriculum.

Introduction — 5 minutes — whole group

Put over the points made in the box below.

> Usually we are in the habit of starting with an activity and then analyzing its curricular strengths! This time, I am asking you to devise an activity to work towards a particular Attainment Target within the National Curriculum.

Implementation — 55 minutes — small and whole groups

1. Workshop — Devising activities for particular developmental levels — 20 minutes — small group
   For this activity you will need to select specific Attainment Targets from either the Science or Design and Technology documents.
   Considerable help will be required here since working this way round is unfamiliar to most teachers. Be prepared to give considerable support to this workshop.
2. Workshop — Assessing levels of achievement using criteria — 20 minutes — small group
   You will need to establish the meaning of criterion-referenced statements. It is likely that most teachers will be unfamiliar with their use let alone in devising them. Again, considerable help will be required.
3. Discussion — 15 minutes — whole group
   Use this opportunity to clarify issues and develop individuals.

Assessing Children's Science and Design Technology Level

Workshop 4: Devising and Assessing Activities

1. Workshop — small group activity
    Devising activities for particular developmental levels. Work in pairs.
    1.1 Select a Science Attainment Target which motivates you from the following:
        Types and uses of materials
        Forces
        Electricity and magnetism
        Energy
    1.2 Using the selected Attainment Target for each level (1–6) devise an activity which will help children work towards the appropriate statements of attainment.
2. Workshop — small group activity
    Assessing levels of achievement using criteria. Now for each statement of attainment, work out a set of criteria, say three or four, which will enable you to assess the level of achievement of individuals.
3. Discussion — whole group

Action Tactics 2: Matching, Continuity and Progression

Workshop 1: The Progressive Development of Investigative Skills

Leader's Guide

Having familiarized themselves with the Science Statements of Attainment contained within the checklist, through using it with their own classes, this workshop allows those involved to compare the levels of working of different groups of children.

Introduction — 5 minutes — whole group
Put over the points made in the box below:

> Well, how did it go? Did you all manage to find the time to try out the check list? I do hope so, because what I would like us to do now is to compare the way in which different groups of children tried to solve the 'bouncing ball' problem. Perhaps then we would consider the way in which we might use such a check list in school on a permanent basis.

Implementation — 55 minutes

1. Report back — Bouncing Balls — 40 minutes — whole group
    You will find that, in this part of the session, it is useful to start the report back with the teachers of the youngest children and work progressively through the age range. You will also need to make sure that colleagues:
    (a) make some attempt to assess science level.
    (b) assess individuals rather than groups of children.
    (c) support their assessment with evidence e.g. an observation they have made, an overheard comment or point raised in discussion.
2. Discussion — Skills Progression — 15 minutes — whole group
    Use points made in the report back to raise the issue of progression of development of skills. It is usually possible to highlight stages which follow the checklist quite closely. However, be careful to make the point that such a progression is not necessarily related to age. If appropriate, also try to raise the issue of using the checklist for a trial period with a view to modifying it for use on a more permanent basis.

Matching, Continuity and Progression

Workshop 1: The Progressive Development of Investigative Skills

You will now have been able to try out the 'bouncing ball' activities with a small group of children in your own class. Not only should this have given you experience of using the check list but it should also have provided you with a basis upon which to draw comparisons.

1. Report back — Bouncing Balls
   This is designed to allow you to compare the experiences of colleagues with that of your own.
2. Discussion — skills progression

Action Tactics 2: Matching, Continuity and Progression

Workshop 2: The Progressive Development of Concepts

Leader's Guide

Most teachers are now becoming aware that children acquire the ability to problem solve in several clearly defined stages. Less well known is the notion that the development of concepts also follows a progression as children mature. This workshop is designed to explore this issue.

Introduction — 5 minutes — whole group

Put over the points made in the box below:

Now, I'm sure that you all know the progression for investigative skills off by heart! *No?* Well at least each of you can assess levels of investigative skill development and provide appropriate activities for individual children. However, can you do the same for the development of concepts? This workshop is intended to help you do just that.

Implementation — 55 minutes

1. Workshop — The provision of appropriate activities — 30 minutes — small groups
   Your role in this workshop is to guide the thinking of each group with respect to the provision of *appropriate* activities. Often difficulties are experienced in suggesting work that is specific enough to take children from one stage to another in the progression.
2. Discussion — The provision of appropriate activities to aid progression — 25 minutes — whole group
   Ask each group to report back in turn. Try to draw up a composite list in each case if possible, but try to make sure that each of the concepts are discussed. The quality of your leadership in the workshop will determine the quality of the input to the discussion and, thus, the outcome of the session. Use the suggested activities in the handout to conclude the discussion.

Matching Continuity and Progression

Workshop 2: The Progressive Development of Concepts

You should now be familiar with the stages through which children progress in developing the skills of investigation. Similarly, they also progress through stages when developing concepts.

1. Workshop — The provision of appropriate activities
   Attached are sheets which show the expected progression of development of the concepts of sorting and classifying, life cycle and solution. Work in small groups and decide upon which kinds of activity would be appropriate for children at each of the stages concerned in the progression. Do this for each of the concepts above and transfer your findings to O.H.P. transparency for the discussion.
2. Discussion — The provision of appropriate activities to aid progression

Reference: modified from, *Towards a Science of Science Teaching:*
Cognitive Development and Curriculum Demand
Shayer and Adey (1981), Heinemann Educational Publishers

CONCEPT — Solution

IDEAS AND ABILITIES	APPROPRIATE ACTIVITIES
S/He thinks that the solute simply 'disappears'	
Salt/sugar 'dissolve' in water	
Mass of solute (i.e. global idea of amount) is conserved; but volume is not	
S/He understands that the process is reversible	
Knows that the particles inter-mingle, but 'stay the same', so that each conserves volume, weight and chemical properties	
Knows that saturation involves an equilibrium situation, with precipitation rate = solution rate	

Reference: ***Match and Mismatch*, 'Finding Answers'**
Oliver & Boyd, Longman Group UK Limited

CONCEPT — Sorting and classifying

IDEAS AND ABILITIES	APPROPRIATE ACTIVITIES
Cannot give reasons for putting things together which are consistent with objects in the group	
Forms groups of things which 'go together' rather than all sharing a common property	
Can use the presence or absence of a single feature as a basis for grouping	
Once s/he has sorted objects s/he can resort them according to another criterion which is suggested to her/him, but cannot find one for her/himself	
Can select and use different criteria for resorting the objects in a different way	

Reference: *Match and Mismatch*, 'Finding Answers'
Oliver & Boyd

CONCEPT — Life cycle

IDEAS AND ABILITIES	APPROPRIATE ACTIVITIES
Links 'living' with 'active'; does not regard inactive forms of life as alive	
Considers that eggs come alive when they hatch, and similarly seeds when they sprout	
Recognizes that plants and inactive forms of animals are alive	
Relates some parts of the life cycle to each other, but not to the whole process of reproduction	
Appreciates that living things reproduce themselves through their life cycles, which vary in pattern	
Knows the details of life cycles of some common plants and animals in the environment	

Reference: *Match and Mismatch* , 'Finding Answers'
Oliver & Boyd

Activities which encourage development of ideas about sorting and classifying

The following are some activities which involve classifying and which give opportunity for ideas of classification to develop. In the table which follows, the activities are defined by the numbers which they are given here.

1. Picking out and naming similarities and differences between objects, people, etc., using exhibits on the nature table, toys brought to school, the weather from day to day, etc.
2. Sorting a variety of objects and materials. Discussing reasons for grouping things together, describing why some fit with others, and so on.
3. Dividing objects into two groups according to presence or absence of one aspect, e.g., shells and not-shells, leaves which are green or not green, children who are taller or not taller than I am, etc.
4. Sorting according to different categories of the one property, e.g., different colours or materials or shapes.
5. Sorting according to one property and then re-sorting according to another one which he finds for himself.
6. Applying two criteria at once, e.g., sorting leaves by shape and size.
7. Making and using simple keys.

Reference: *Match and Mismatch*, 'Finding Answers'
Oliver & Boyd

Rough guide to appropriate activities

IDEAS AND ABILITIES	APPROPRIATE ACTIVITIES
Cannot give reasons for putting things together which are consistent with the objects in the group.	1
Forms groups of things which 'go together' rather than all sharing a common property.	1,2,3
Can use the presence or absence of a single feature as a basis for grouping.	1,2,3,4
Once he has sorted objects he can resort them according to another criterion which is suggested to him, but not find one for himself.	2,3,4,5
Can select and use different criteria for resorting the objects in another way.	5,6,7

Reference: *Match and Mismatch*, 'Finding Answers'
Oliver & Boyd

Activities which encourage development of ideas about life cycle

1. Keeping animals and discussing their growth.
2. Examining and planting quick growing seeds, such as mustard and cress. Trying to grow them in different media, seeing what they need to make them grow, talking about what seems to make them grow best.
3. Watching eggs hatch — poultry eggs in an incubator, or snails' eggs in an aquarium, silk-worm eggs, frog spawn, etc.
4. Growing bulbs and corms in pots, flowers from seed in window boxes or a garden plot.
5. Collecting eggs, larvae and pupae, keeping them in suitable conditions and observing changes.
6. Breeding insects throughout a whole life cycle, e.g. ladybirds.
7. Observing parts of life cycles of different creatures, e.g. bees, ants, snails, and supplementing with information from books.
8. Germinating large seeds and studying details of growth.
9. Studying details of breeding in mammals and widening knowledge of different life cycles.

Reference: *Match and Mismatch* , 'Finding Answers'
Oliver & Boyd

Rough guide to appropriate activities

IDEAS AND ABILITIES	APPROPRIATE ACTIVITIES
Links 'living' with 'active'; does not regard inactive forms of life as alive.	1,2,3
Considers that eggs come alive when they hatch, and similarly seeds when they sprout	1,2,3,4
Recognizes that plants and inactive forms of animals are alive.	1,2,3,4,5
Relates some parts of the life cycle to each other, but not to the whole process of reproduction	1,2,3,4,5,6
Appreciates that living things reproduce themselves through their life cycles, which vary in pattern	1,2,3,4,5,6,7
Knows the details of life cycles of some common plants and animals in the environment	1,2,3,4,5,6,7,8,9

Action Tactics 2: Matching, Continuity and Progression

Workshop 3: Identifying a Conceptual Progression

Leader's Guide

This workshop is designed to provide teachers with the opportunity to try to identify at first hand, the stages involved in the development of the concept of 'Pollution'.

Introduction — 5 minutes — whole group

Put over the points made in the box below:

> In the last workshop we had the conceptual progression worked out for us. However, for most, the research work has just not been carried out and so we have to rely on ourselves to work something out. Here is some work for you to analyze — the children were all aged 10.

Implementation — 55 minutes

1. Workshop — The concept of 'Pollution' — 40 minutes — small groups
   1.1 Try to ensure that each group writes down *statements* which can be supported by *evidence*.
   1.2 You will need to provide quite a bit of help here giving particular attention to statements which are questionable. The first chart will help you here.
2. Discussion — The progressive development of ideas about pollution — 15 minutes — whole group
   As well as considering this primary concept, it might also be useful to discuss some of the secondary ideas raised (see the second chart) together with the skills being developed and the knowledge acquired.

CHILD	PRIMARY CONCEPT						
	Pollution as: harmful waste gases/materials in the air	dirt which can be collected on filter paper	being proportional to the age of the car	being proportional to the size of the car	being regarded as dirt stored by the car	being affected by choke	being related to make of the car
1	✓						
2		✓					
3							
4			✓	✓	✓		
5			✓	✓	✓		✓
6						✓	
7	✓	✓					

CHILD	SECONDARY CONCEPTS			INVESTIGATIVE SKILLS			KNOWLEDGE	
	Exhaust as: a means of escape of waste gases/ materials	Choke as: a means of regulating air/petrol mix	a means of burning more petrol	Making observations	Making predictions	Drawing conclusions	Pollution is harmful	Car facts
1	✓	✓	✓	✓			✓	
2	✓			✓			✓	✓
3	✓			✓	✓			✓
4					✓			✓
5				✓	✓			
6		✓	✓	✓		✓		✓
7								

Matching, Continuity and Progression
Workshop 3: Identifying a Conceptual Progression

In the last workshop developmental progression for three concepts were provided. Whilst much research is currently being undertaken, developmental progressions for some concepts are not readily available and it is up to individual teachers to identify the stages involved.

1. Workshop — the concept of 'Pollution'
   You are provided with examples of children's work on the concept of pollution.
   1.1 Using the written work only as a guide, work in small groups and consider what the teacher is learning about each of the children concerned. Try to obtain evidence from the observations which will enable you to make an assessment of where each child is with respect to his ideas about pollution.
   1.2 Now try to use the evidence to make a developmental progression for the concept of pollution. Transfer to an O.H.P. transparency for the discussion.
2. Discussion — The progressive development of ideas about pollution.

The Concept of Pollution: Children's Work
(Please note that the original spelling has been retained throughout.)

Child 1.

Pollution from cars

The car exhaust gives out the waste gases and dirt from the engin. These gases and dirt can be harmful and cause what we call pollution. We tested for pollution by doing some experiments we stuck filter paper on a ruler and asked some of the teachers if they could start their cars up to warm them up. Then we got the filter paper and put it at the open sideof the car exhaust. we put it there for one minute. we did tvo filter papers one filter paper was without choke and the other paper was with choke. The chok is for more petrol to go into the engine to help it warm up quicer.

Child 2.

Pollution

When we went out to test for pollution in cars from our school we found that lots of oil came out from the exhaust. We wrote about the cars and put a piece of filter paper near the exhaust to see how much pollution there was from the cars we did 2 test on each car 1 test shows pollution from cars with the choke and the second to show pollution from cars with out the choke some cars do not have a choke like Mrs Barrtt so she has to fuel enjected. When we tested we had to stand away from the exhaust because it is bad for you.

Child 3.

Pollution

Mrs W's car was the worst. I would think it would be the one with a clean engine because it is less than a year old. Mr. A say's perhaps it isnt the age of the car that matter's. Every car that has a exhaust and is three year's old needs a new one. As pollution is coming out of the exhaust.

Mrs X
Car: Volvo
number plate: MVD88L
Colour: Sea Green
Licence: 22634235
Age: 10 years old
Tyres: Turbo steel

Mrs Y
Car: Kadett
Colour: Light Blue
Licence: 31135825
Number plate: SPP141R
Age: 8 years old

Mrs Z
Car: Astra
Licence: 30799082
Number plate: GVS433Y
Colour: Brown
Age: 1 year

Child 4.

Pollution from Car's

I think that an old car will give off more dirt than a new one's because the old car's have more time to collect. The filter paper I think will get a lot of dirt from the old car, and start to burn. The new car's will not give off as much dirt.

The Cavalier I think will give off quite a lot of pollution because it is big. I think the estate will be exactly the same. The mini would not store much dirt for the simple reason it is very small.

by Helen

Mrs U
Car: Cavalier
Age: 3year's
Registration number: LKO431V
Licence: 2265167
Colour: Orange
Not much dirt collected from exoaust
lenght of time 1.00

Miss V
Car: Marina
Colour: Dark green
Licence number: 31138349
Registration number: LUR80P
Age: 8 years

Mr A
Car: Christa
Colour: Dark red
Licence: 383401107104
Number plate: SBM542R

Child 5.

Pollution from cars.

I think that the filter paper will turn black and dirty and I also think that old cars will give more pollution because it cus has been used more and cars that are new has not enough time to get dirty. The cavalier I think will give a lot of pollution because it is very big and I think that the mine will give a lot of pollution but not as much as the cavalier. I also think that a rolls royce won't give alot of pollution.

Child 6.

We are doing thie experiment to find out how much pollution we would get out of holding a piece of filter paper to the exhaust of a car for one minute. We first tested the exhaust with choke and then without choke. When the choke is out it helps the engine to start easier. We think more people use a choke in the winter than in the summer. We think more people use the choke in winter because it helps the petrol and oil run faster into the engine. The petrol has to run faster because the engine is cold and it warms up the car. When the choke is out it burns more petrol and oil. When the choke is out (it) we think it makes the filter paper more dirty because more petrol and oil is being burnt at a time.

Mirs W	Mirs V	Mirs X	Mr A	Mr B
Make vauxhall		volvo	Ford	Ford
Name Astra	Marina	volvo	Chrysler	Van
Colour Brown	Green	green	red	blue
Age 1 year	10 yrs.	13 yrs.	9 yrs.	11 yrs.
Registanon				
GVS 433Y	LWR 380P	MWD 88L	sbm 542R	Hnk 532N

Child 7.

our second test was to put two trays outside, one near a main road and one away from the road. The reason we are leaving the two trays out is because we want to see how much pollution there is in the air. We have got blotting paper to see how much dirt collects in the trays. I said that we should leave the trays out for an hour but were having it out for two hours to give the dirt time to collect.

Action Tactics 2: Matching, Continuity and Progression

Workshop 4: Matching

Leader's Guide

Even though teachers have a 'gut feeling' about the levels of development of individuals, they are often reluctant to make special provision and fall back into 'safety' of a whole class approach. This workshop tries to force this issue, at the same time, making the point that it is not so difficult as it seems once the idea is accepted.

Introduction — 5 minutes — whole group

Put over the points made in the box below:

> Well done! I am now quite confident that most of you are happy enough with the Science Statements of Attainment for investigative skills (check list) to enable you to use it in your classrooms. Unfortunately, this is only the first stage. Can you now use it to provide activities for individual children that will match their abilities? Only if you can do this will you help them to progress in their thinking.

Implementation— 55 minutes

1. Workshop — Matching — 25 minutes — small group
    If possible, arrange your groups according to the age range taught. In this way you are more likely to obtain a progression overall whilst still enabling staff to work over the complete ability range.
2. Discussion — Maximizing a child's potential — 30 minutes — whole group
    Invite feedback from each group in turn making sure that the statements they make relate directly to the check list. (Science A.T. 1 statements of Attainment for Investigative Skills; see workshop 'Introducing a Criterion-Referenced Checklist).

Matching, Continuity and Progression

Workshop 4: Matching

Having identified the 'Science level' of an individual child, it is important that you are able to provide that child with an activity which will extend his or her thinking so that progression, i.e. development in problem solving ability, can take place.

1. Workshop — 'Matching'
    Now assume you have a mixed ability group of four children who wish to examine the problem you investigated earlier, 'Tip Top'. If necessary, how would you guide them so that John (Science A.T. 1 — level 1), Mary (Science A.T. 1 — level 3), Catherine (Science A.T. 1 — level 6) and Phillip (Science A.T. 1 — level 4) could work at their maximum potential.
2. Discussion — Maximizing a child's potential

Action Tactics 2: Matching Continuity and Progression

Workshop 5: Planning a Differentiated Topic

Leader's Guide

Crucial to the implementation of any topic is the need to provide a differentiated curriculum. The National Curriculum Statements of Attainment can be used as a guide when planning.

Introduction — 5 minutes — whole group

Put over the points made in the box below:

> Now I'm sure that you'll all be delighted to have some help in planning your topics! This is just what this workshop allows us to do — by working together we can quickly build up a permanent resource for use in school.

Implementation — 85 minutes

1. Discussion — 5 minutes — whole group
   Be prepared to apply some pressure here in selecting a topic. It is important to start the workshop and come to grips with the problem rather than spending too much time at the outset. Do not let this session overrun.
2. Workshop — 65 minutes — groups of two or three
   Colleagues may need considerable help here so it is a good idea to have plenty of teacher/pupil materials available to give them ideas. You should also use the exemplar charts which have been filled in for the 'Movement' Topic together with the National Curriculum Statements of Attainment. You will see the Statements of Attainment have been coded: 3.3 refers to the third Statement of Attainment at level three for a particular Attainment Target.
3. Discussion — 15 minutes — whole group
   It is important here to iron out any areas of overlap since, in this instance, each activity and in particular, the pupil material, should be targeted at a particular level.

TOPIC	Movement			SUBJECT
			LEVEL 3	**Science**
			3	

A.T. Number	A.T. Level	Statement of Attainment
1	3.1 to 3.9	The Attainment Target reached will depend upon the nature of the activity
2	3.3	Know that living things respond to (daily) changes
3	3.1	Know that basic life processes e.g. movement are common to human beings and other living things
10	3.1	Understand that when things are changed in shape, begin to move or stop moving, forces are acting on them.
10	3.2	Understand the factors which cause objects to float or sink in water.
11	3.2	Understand that a complete circuit is needed for an electrical device such as a bulb or buzzer to work.
12	3.2	Know that information can be stored electrically e.g. graphics
12	3.3	Be able to select information stored on a computer e.g. graphics
13	3.1	Understand, in qualitative terms, that models and machines need a source of energy in order to work
13	3.3	Be able to use simple power sources (electric motors, rubber bands) and devices which transform energy (gears, belts, levers)

A.T. Number	LEVEL	DESCRIPTION OF ACTIVITY	Pupil/Teacher Material	A.T. 1								
				3.1	3.2	3.3	3.4	3.5	3.6	3.7	3.8	3.9
3 2	3.1 3.3	*Minibeast Movement* Study of minibeast movement in relation to surface, environmental conditions e.g. food, humidity		/	–	/	/	/	/	/	/	/
3 10 12 12	3.1 3.1 3.2 3.3	*Human Movement* Study of human movement measuring time taken, distance, force etc. and logging the data on computer. Compare results with different ages.		/	/	/	/	/	/	/	/	/
10 12 12	3.1 3.2 3.3	*Vehicular Movement* A study of the force required to move a stationary object or vehicle with or without rollers or wheels on different surfaces and logging data obtained.		/	?	–	–	–	/	/	/	/
10	3.2	*Movement on water* Floating and sinking activities with plasticine boats and other objects.		/	–	/	/	/	/	/	/	/
10 10 11 13 13	3.1 3.2 3.2 3.1 3.3	*Movement on water* The production and testing of model boats using a variety of sources of power.		/	–	/	/	/	/	/	/	/
10 11 13 13	3.1 3.2 3.1 3.3	*Movement on land* The production and testing of a variety of vehicles using a variety of sources of power.		/	/	/	/	/	/	/	/	/
10	3.1	*Movement in the air/water* Simple studies of 'lift' and 'drag' (using fluid flow equipment).		/	–	/	/	–	/	–	/	/
10 13	3.1 3.1	*Movement in the air* The production and testing of simple model planes including parachutes etc.		/	–	/	/	/	/	/	/	/

Matching, Continuity and Progression

Workshop 5: Planning a Differentiated Topic

Provided adequate planning takes place, it should be possible to build up resources for a number of topic areas which work towards the Statements of Attainment in the National Curriculum.

1. Discussion — whole group
   Identify, as a group, a topic which you would like to develop.
2. Workshop — small groups
   2.1 Now divide into small groups and using the first page of the framework provided, identify the Attainment Targets which could be worked towards through the selected topic.
   2.2 Now select a level at which you would like to develop the work. You will need to take into account the span of levels within which you are expected to develop the National Curriculum in your particular phase. Each group should select a different level.
   2.3 Identify the particular Statements of Attainment which apply at the level at which you are working and enter them into the chart.
   2.4 You are now in a position to devise activities which work towards particular Statements of Attainment. Enter these onto the second page of the framework together with any reference to pupil teacher material. Also, you may find that any one activity may be used to work towards several Attainment Targets. These can also be identified and entered on to the chart as a cross reference.
3. Discussion — whole group
   Now is the time to combine ideas and deal with any areas of overlap.

| TOPIC | | LEVEL 3 _____ | SUBJECT _____ |

A.T. Number	A.T. Level	Statement of Attainment
1		The Attainment Target reached will depend upon the nature of the activity

A.T. Number	LEVEL	DESCRIPTION OF ACTIVITY	Pupil/Teacher Material	A.T. 1

Action Tactic 2: Curriculum Balance

Workshop 1: Curriculum Analysis

Leader's Guide

Traditionally, in most schools, teachers have been required to provide a forecast of the topic work they intended to implement, but little thought was given either to how this reflected ideas about science and design technology or how they fitted into the wider curriculum of the school. An understanding of how each topic might reflect school policy, even if there was one was certainly not required. Now the situation has changed and it is widely recognized that some framework for curriculum planning is desirable. This workshop is concerned with the curriculum analysis upon which such a framework can be based. In this instance it features science but a similar analysis can clearly be carried out for design technology or another area of the curriculum.

Introduction — 5 minutes — whole group

Put over the points made in the box below:

> What topic are you doing next term? How was this decided? Was there any discussion with colleagues? How does your topic link in with science work in other year groups/the school? Do you think it should? What can we do about it?

Implementation— 55 minutes

1. Workshop — Topic identification — 15 minutes — individual and year groups
   It is important that colleagues have done their homework here and that a number of topics, implemented over a number of years, are available for analysis.
2. Workshop — Topic analysis — 40 minutes — year groups
   You may well need to explore the meaning of the word 'concept' and certainly explore the nature of individual ideas. The National Curriculum Statements of Attainment are invaluable here. Also, the Teachers Guide of Longmans' *Science World* and the APU concept statements at age 11 years are of help also. Certainly you will need to emphasize that, in spite of the language, the ideas can be quite simple in the early stages.

   A positive outcome of the aspect of the workshop is that it reinforces what is *actually* being accomplished in school and, because of this, is less threatening than it would otherwise seem.

Curriculum Balance

Workshop 1: Curriculum Analysis

How do *you* decide which topic you will explore with your class? Perhaps it is one of their choosing, perhaps it reflects your own particular interest. Do you take your choice of topic into account when considering balance in terms of the design/technology and science curriculum of particular year groups and the whole school?

1. Workshop — Topic identification
   1.1 Individually make a list of topics/content which you would normally teach to your class during the year. The topics listed should be those you use on a regular basis but could also include those you use less frequently or those you would like to introduce at a later date.
   1.2 Come together as year groups and identify the topics/content normally included in the curriculum of your particular year.
2. Workshop — Topic analysis
   Finally, enter the topics/content for each year group on the grid and check the appropriate spaces to complete your initial conceptual analysis of the curriculum in your school.

PRIMARY SCIENCE
ATTAINMENT TARGET/TOPIC GRID

	TOPIC / Attainment Target		Year 1	Year 2	Year 3	Year 4
Exploration of Science	1	Exploration of Science				
	2	The Variety of Life 3				
	3	Processes of Life 3				
	6	Types and uses of materials 3				
	8	Explaining how materials behave 3				
	9	Earth and Atmosphere 3				
	13	Energy 3				
Knowledge and Understanding of Science	4	Genetics and Evolution 2				
	7	Making new materials 2				
	11	Electricity and Magnetism 2				
	5	Human influences on the Earth 1				
	10	Forces 1				
	12	Information technology 1				
	14	Sound and Music 1				
	15	Using light and electro-magnetic radiation 1				
	16	The Earth in Space 1				
	17	The Nature of Science 1				

3, 2, and 1 = Relative weightings

Action Tactics 2: Curriculum Balance

Workshop 2: Curriculum Review

Leader's Guide

Having carried out a curriculum analysis, it is now possible to consider the contribution of individuals and year groups to the whole school curriculum. Using this information, it is then possible to construct a framework within which the issues of curriculum balances, continuity and progression can be addressed.

Introduction — 5 minutes — whole group

Put over the points made in the box below:

> Now you have completed your analysis, the tedious bit, you are ready to reap your rewards! How balanced is the work you are already involved in? Are there any gaps? If so — where? You will be surprised at the quality of the work you are already doing, *but* don't become too complacent! The workshop will tell you why.

Implementation — 55 minutes — whole group

1. Workshop — Curriculum review — 40 minutes — whole group
   The data can be analyzed in four ways:
   1.1 personally, to identify strength and weaknesses of individuals.
   1.2 in year groups, to analyze equality of experience.
   1.3 in terms of the total age range, to identify the total and partal 'gaps'.
   1.4 in terms of the total age range to investigate opportunities for progression and continuity of experience.
2. Discussion — An appropriate curriculum — 15 minutes — whole group
   Without being prescriptive, it should be possible to select a number of topics which lend themselves to the development of a number of important Attainment Targets which can be worked towards progressively, from year to year. Ideally, it should be possible to compile a list of topics, from which teachers can select, which will allow progression in each of the four major areas (materials, energy, forces and living things).

Curriculum Balance
Workshop 2: Curriculum Review

This workshop should help you highlight your own strengths and weaknesses, as well as identifying areas of concern on a whole school basis.

1. Workshop — Curriculum Review
   1.1 Attainment Targets
      (a) Which Attainment Targets are being considered in all the year groups?
      (b) Are there any Attainment Targets which *should* be considered by all the year groups?
      (c) Are there any gaps?
      (d) Is it possible for children to progress in their development of ideas?
   1.2 Topics/Content
      (a) What overlap is there?
      (b) What can you do to prevent this?
      (c) Are the topics in each year group appropriate to the age range?
      (d) Have any important topics been missed out?
      (e) Can you resource the ones selected?
2. Discussion — An appropriate curriculum
   After considering the questions posed above, you should be able to come to some agreement concerning the Attainment Targets and topics/content you wish to make available for study. Ideally, for each year group, you should compile a topic/content list from which teachers can select.

Index